CRIMINAL PROCEDURE SIMULATIONS

By
Michael Vitiello
McGeorge School of Law

BRIDGE TO PRACTICE

WEST®
A Thomson Reuters business

Mat #41166340

© 2012 Thomson Reuters

610 Opperman Drive
St. Paul, MN 55123
1–800–313–9378

Printed in the United States of America

ISBN: 978–0–314–27641–4

ACKNOWLEDGEMENTS

Special thanks go to my acquisitions editors Trina Tinglum and Louis Higgins. The proposal for the Simulation Series was in front of another publisher for several months when I submitted it to West at Trina's suggestion. Within a few days of receiving the proposal, Louis questioned me about the proposal with insight and intensity. My offer to publish the series came within a matter of a few days.

I am also appreciative for the excellent research assistance provided by Pacific McGeorge student R.J. Cooper; for thoughtful and supportive comments from former prosecutors Eden Forsythe (and former research assistant) and Cliff Gessner and from Professors Joshua Dressler and George Thomas. I am also appreciative of support from many of my Pacific McGeorge colleagues who are considering publishing books in the Simulation Series, especially John Sprankling, whose book on Property will be forthcoming in 2012. I also wish to thank Pacific McGeorge librarian Michele Finerty for considerable help in locating an array of documents, Faculty Support staff member R.K. Van Every for her help with solving any number of technical problems, Faculty Support staff members Wendy Owens and Kristi Axtell for helping me create various documents, and Lori Hall for putting together the realistic photo array in Chapter Nine. Thanks also go to my colleagues Larry Levine, Jay Leach, John Myers, Ed Telfeyan, and Greg Weber for allowing me to use their photos as part of the chapter on lineups and photo arrays. I feared that they would not look sufficiently like real criminals, but they came through for me as you can assess by examining the photo array in Chapter Nine.

Finally I am especially appreciative of input from my colleague Cary Bricker for her input and help in "beta" testing several simulations.

INTRODUCTION

I. Some Background

Legal education in America has always been schizophrenic: should we educate lawyers experientially through apprenticeships? Or, as is the case in many European countries, should legal education focus on theory and philosophy?

Even after states moved from having lawyers "read the law," whereby would-be lawyers served apprenticeships, to requiring more formal studies in law schools, many law schools treated the study of the law as a vocation. For much of the twentieth century, lower ranked law schools attempted to upgrade their programs to emulate more prestigious schools, which emphasized theory. Indeed, those of us who went to law school in the 1970's remember the frequent refrain that we would acquire skills in practice, not in law school.

Over time, some lawyers, judges, students and professors lamented the lack of practical skills training in law schools. Most law schools responded with the creation of clinics that allow students to learn the application of legal rules to real cases. But despite their popularity in many schools, clinics remain expensive and available to limited numbers of students. Efforts at broad curricular reform have largely fallen by the wayside.

Legal education may be changing. In 2007, the Carnegie Foundation's *Educating Lawyers: Preparation for the Profession of Law* was published. *Educating Lawyers* recognized that the standard first-year curriculum is good at helping students to think like lawyers and provides sufficient academic knowledge and development. But the report faulted the curriculum for failing to go the next step and teaching law students to act like lawyers. It criticized law schools for the separation of theoretical learning from practical skills training.

The report compared legal and medical education, which incorporates clinical or experiential learning into students' formal education.[1] The report argued that such an implementation would be beneficial because the purpose of all professional education, legal and otherwise, is to serve in the place of an apprenticeship. The traditional purpose of an apprenticeship is not merely the academic advancement of the new practitioners, but also the practical development of the skills necessary to be proficient.

---

1. Legal educators use "experiential learning" to mean somewhat different things. For some, it is clinical education. More broadly, however, the term also includes classroom simulation exercises. Classroom exercises have a number of advantages over clinical learning: most importantly, a professor can design material that teaches a fixed set of skills. Whether a student gets a particular set of experiences in a clinical setting is a matter of chance.

The timing of *Educating Lawyers* was critical. In the past, other reports like the McCrate Report in the 1980's have urged greater experiential learning but did not have a dramatic impact on legal education. Coming at a time when legal educators have paid more attention to educational learning theory, *Educating Lawyers* has had an immediate effect. Responding to the Carnegie Report, a number of prominent law schools announced substantial curricular changes to increase experiential learning opportunities for their students. Conferences on implementing the report have proliferated.

A second important factor that, I hope, makes this kind of book timely and valuable is the change in the job market for entry level lawyers. Although the trend began before the economic downturn in 2008, corporate clients of large law firms have resisted paying additional fees for associates. They have challenged one of the traditions of the legal profession, the mentoring of junior lawyers by senior lawyers. That practice is now considered too expensive. That is so not only because of resistance from large clients, but also because, unlike an earlier era, young lawyers no longer make long term commitments to their firms. Thus, by the time a firm recoups the cost of training a new associate, the now-experienced lawyer moves to a new position. Further, when they do hire recent graduates, they want new associates to provide "value added" immediately.

During the summer of 2011, the Association of American Law Schools hosted an event in Seattle. The Association advertised the Conference on the Future of the Law School Curriculum in urgent terms: "We are at a pivotal moment in the history of legal education." Forces from inside and outside the academy are calling for changes in the law school curriculum. One suggested area of change was greater incorporation of experiential learning into the traditional curriculum.

One way in which legal educators can respond to the demand for graduates who can add value to their employers sooner rather than later is by having them develop practical skills from the beginning of their legal careers. Rather than training students in abstract concepts, for example, those of us in the academy should teach our students how to apply those concepts in realistic settings.

That is the purpose of this and similar books in West's Simulation Series. This book is designed for students enrolled in a Criminal Procedure course. This book consists of nine simulations, covering a wide array of issues arising under the Fourth Amendment, the Fifth Amendment, and Sixth Amendment taught in the basic Criminal Procedure course. Today, given the wealth of case law in those areas, most Criminal Procedure professors have limited their coverage to the issues arising during police investigation of crimes. I describe the simulations and different approaches that professors may take in using this material below.

II. *Some Specific Goals of this Book*

This book consists of nine simulations. In determining the topics to cover, I consulted with Criminal Procedure professors around the country and confirmed that their course coverage largely mirrors mine. For example, I cover the application of the guarantees in the Bill of Rights to the States through the process of selective incorporation (usually the first or second chapter in major casebooks). By necessity, I spend about half the semester covering the Fourth Amendment. Thereafter, I cover confessions, first by exploring rules governing voluntary confessions and then, of course, *Miranda* and its progeny. I also cover the Sixth Amendment cases involving police efforts to deliberately elicit statements from defendants after their right to counsel has attached. Finally, I cover issues of standing, fruit-of-the-poison-ous-tree, and inevitable discovery. I have incorporated most of those issues into the various simulation exercises. I have also included a simulation on pre-trial identification procedures, a subject that some professors are able to cover in the basic Criminal Procedure course.

I have created a number of kinds of activities in this book. The first simulation, found in Chapter One, places you in the role of junior counsel to an attorney about to argue a case to the United States Supreme Court. Your job is to help your boss decide how to argue the case. Assessing the various arguments requires you to balance theory with pragmatics.

Many of the other exercises consist of transcripts of oral arguments before trial judges, who have heard motions to suppress the evidence. Based on the record, you will make an oral argument to the judge. Because the court has yet to make factual findings, you may be able to urge the court to find facts in your favor. Lacking demeanor evidence, you may nonetheless be able to argue which version of the facts (one supporting your legal position) is more plausible. For example, a witness's testimony may be inconsistent with another witness's testimony or internally inconsistent or inconsistent with other established facts in the record. The main part of your argument should focus on how the relevant legal rules apply to the facts before the court. That requires close attention to the cases in your casebook.

In addition to transcripts, in two chapters, I have included warrants. That introduces you to the different procedure applicable when the defendant has challenged the sufficiency of a warrant as opposed to the legality of a warrantless arrest or search. Those assignments also require you to focus on the sufficiency of legal documents.

Throughout this book, I use the widely adopted version of dates. For example, instead of using a date like March 10, 2011, I use March 10, YR–00. That avoids the text from becoming chronologically obsolete. YR–00 refers to the current year; YR–01 to the previous year; YR–01, to two years ago; YR–03, to three years ago.

In the Teacher's Manual available to your professor, I also provide other suggestions in some of the chapters. For example, in some instances, the simulation lends itself to a short writing assignment. Your professor may have you draft a memorandum of points and authorities supporting one side or the other of the argument. Further, in one chapter, the Teacher's Manual includes a trial court opinion, resolving the legal issues. Your professor may have you draft a short appellate argument or argue before an appellate panel, urging that the court affirm or reverse the trial court.

Finally, I have created role summaries in two of the chapters. Chapter Three: Vehicle Searches includes role summaries for two officers and a tow truck driver and relevant legal documents. The Teacher's Manual for Chapter Nine: Lineups, One-on-one Show-Ups and Photo Arrays includes role summaries for some of the victims of a robbery. Your professor may assign students as counsel and as witnesses. In those simulations, you will have the opportunity to examine or cross-examine a witness and use your knowledge of the law of Evidence to get relevant documents or physical items admitted into the record.

Large classes are a reality of law school. Most professors have few additional resources like teaching assistants. In a course like Criminal Procedure, professors must cover a large amount of material. In the typical classroom, professors may be hard-pressed to assign all of the simulation exercises or to provide an opportunity for every student to participate. If so, I would urge you to volunteer to participate when the opportunity arises. The Teacher's Manual includes various suggestions for how your professor may integrate these exercises into a traditional class room. There, I offer some thoughts on how a professor may be able to provide every student with an opportunity to learn by doing. That is the ultimate goal of this book.

Good luck!

TABLE OF CONTENTS

——————

CRIMINAL PROCEDURE SIMULATIONS

BRIDGE TO PRACTICE

CHAPTER ONE

SELECTIVE INCORPORATION

I. INTRODUCTION

The simulation exercise in this chapter gives you an opportunity to explore how the Supreme Court expanded its authority over state criminal proceedings. Framed differently, it explores how specific protections found in the Bill of Rights became limitations on state power.

This chapter consists of a brief overview of the relevant law. It then provides a short exercise. That exercise requires you to make some strategic choices about how to argue a case before the United States Supreme Court.

II. OVERVIEW OF THE LAW

Most Criminal Procedure casebooks include a discussion of how specific protections in the Bill of Rights have become applicable as limitations on state power. They do so at a minimum because the text of the Bill of Rights is far from clear on whether the various protections found there were intended as limitations on state power and because the case law reveals a good deal about constitutional evolution.

Commentators largely agree that the Bill of Rights was originally intended to limit federal, not state, power. The First Amendment ("Congress shall make no law ...") suggests as much, but other amendments do not include similar language. Despite that, the history surrounding the adoption of the Constitution and Bill of Rights supports the conclusion that the Bill of Rights was not intended to limit states' power. The framers and the public were largely concerned with granting the newly created federal government too much power. Further, states had their own bills of rights in their constitutions—indeed, many of the protections found in the Bill of Rights were modeled on state constitutional provisions.

Writing for the Court in *Barron v. Baltimore,* 32 U.S. (7 Pet.) 243 (1833), Chief Justice Marshall stated that the Bill of Rights "contain[s] no expression indicating an intention to apply them to the State governments." *Barron* settled the matter prior to adoption of the Fourteenth Amendment.

Whatever else the Fourteenth Amendment was intended to do, it clearly limited state power. It contains two provisions relevant to the question posed in this simulation exercise. It states that no state "shall abridge the privileges and immunities of citizens of the United States ..." It also states that no state shall "deprive any person of life, liberty, or property, without due process of law ..."

With regard to the question posed in this exercise, some justices and commentators have argued that the intent of the Fourteenth Amendment was to incorporate all of the protections found in the Bill of Rights and to apply them to the states. For some, the specific protections in the Bill of Rights are among those privileges possessed by citizens of the United States. A second argument is that the Fourteenth Amendment Due Process Clause includes the freedoms secured by the Bill of Rights.

The Court effectively rejected the first argument in *The Slaughter–House Cases*, 83 U.S. (6 Wall.) 36 (1873). The discussion in *The Slaughter–House Cases* was dicta and the Court was closely divided. But in subsequent cases, the Court rejected the theory. The Court's privileges and immunity case law leaves open a number of questions: for example, it is not entirely clear what federal rights are guaranteed under that clause. While *The Slaughter–House Cases* remain intact, more contemporary scholars have argued that the Fourteenth Amendment's "privileges and immunities" provision did intend to make the protections in the Bill of Rights applicable to the states.

Students familiar with modern criminal procedural cases like *Miranda v. Arizona* may have trouble realizing how limited the Court's involvement was in reviewing state criminal convictions until the Warren Court era, effectively between 1961 and 1968. Its early interventions involved instances of racial injustice in the South. For example, in *Powell v. Alabama*, 287 U.S. 45 (1932), the Court overturned the death sentences imposed on defendants, young African-American men, who were accused of raping two white women. The basis of the decision was narrow: on the facts of the case (e.g., uneducated youths, faced with capital charges, far from home, unable to afford counsel), the Court found that their convictions violated Due Process.

Even more startling were the facts in *Brown v. Mississippi*, 297 U.S. 278 (1936). There, a sheriff's deputy admitted to beating one of the suspects in order to secure a confession. As in *Powell*, the defendants' convictions led to the imposition of the death penalty. The State argued that the Fifth Amendment right against self-incrimination did not apply to the states. While the Court agreed, again, the basis of the decision, reversing the convictions, was the Due Process Clause.

As long ago as the 1880's, the Court rejected a defendant's claim that the Fifth Amendment's requirement of a grand jury indictment was binding on the states. *Hurtado v. California*, 110 U.S. 516 (1884). In dicta, the Court suggested that some of the protections in the Bill of Rights might be necessary to guarantee a defendant fundamental fairness.

For many years, the Court effectively adopted that approach. In one case after another, the Court rejected the defendant's claim that the state violated specific provisions of the Bill of Rights and held that a federal court should overturn a state criminal conviction only if the state procedure offended a "principle of justice so rooted in the traditions and conscience of our people as to be ranked as fundamental." *Twining v. New Jersey,* 211 U.S. 78, 114 (1908).

The Court's Due Process jurisprudence was open to criticism. As Justice Black argued in his famous *Adamson* dissent, "fundamental fairness" invites the Court to substitute "its own concepts of decency and fundamental justice for the language of the Bill of Rights." *Adamson v. California,* 332 U.S. 46 (1947). By contrast, Justice Black argued that the intent of the Fourteenth Amendment was to make all of the guarantees in the Bill of Rights applicable as limitations to state power. His "total incorporation" theory never secured a majority among the justices.

Instead, the approach taken by the Warren Court arrived at almost the same place and dramatically changed the course of criminal procedure through a process called selective incorporation. Effectively beginning in 1961 with *Mapp v. Ohio,* 367 U.S. 643 (1961), the Court found that almost of all of the protections in the Bill of Rights are applicable to the states. It did so on a right-by-right basis. Unlike the fundamental fairness approach in cases like *Powell,* the inquiry did not focus on the facts of the case before the Court. Instead, the Court focused on the particular guarantee and asked whether it was fundamental to an Anglo–American scheme of justice. Previously, the Court asked more generally whether the right was fundamental to the scheme of ordered liberty. The result of the Court's selective incorporation cases has been to federalize criminal procedure. Indeed, prior to the 1960's, law schools did not have a separate course on Criminal Procedure. The few constitutional cases were taught in Constitutional Law and some procedural doctrines like venue and jurisdiction might find their way into a basic Criminal Law casebook.

The difference between selective incorporation and fundamental fairness can be illustrated by the last important Warren Court incorporation decision, *Duncan v. Louisiana,* 391 U.S. 145 (1968). *Duncan* held that the Sixth Amendment right to a jury trial was fully applicable to the states. The opinion spent no time questioning whether Duncan received a fair trial, as it would have done under a fundamental fairness analysis. After the Warren Court years, the Court occasionally addressed incorporation; but by 1968, the Court had incorporated almost all of the guarantees in the Bill of Rights.

While this history is fascinating to many of us, it is not only of historical significance as was demonstrated when the Supreme Court decided *District of Columbia v. Heller,* 554 U.S. 570 (2008), during the 2007 term. There, the Court found that the Second Amendment created a personal right to bear arms. Because the law involved was federal, the Court did not have to decide whether the Second Amendment also limited the power of the states to regulate individuals' rights to bear arms. That was the issue in *McDonald v. Chicago,* 561 U.S. 3025 (2010). The issue divided the Court and resulted in a 5–4 ruling. As developed below, this simulation exercise requires you to consider some strategic choices that counsel for McDonald faced when he argued to the Court.

III. THEORY OR PRACTICE?

For purposes of this simulation, you are an associate to the senior partner of a law firm. The senior partner is about to argue on behalf of McDonald in *McDonald v. Chicago.* The senior partner has asked for your thoughts on two specific questions. The first is whether, in light of recent scholarship suggesting that *The Slaughter–House Cases* were wrongly decided, the partner should argue that the intent of the Fourteenth Amendment was to incorporate all of the guarantees in the Bill of Rights (essentially, Justice Black's position)? The partner hands you the following excerpt from Justice Black's *Adamson* dissent:

> ... I am attaching to this dissent, an appendix which contains a resume, by no means complete, of the [Fourteenth] Amendment's history. In my judgment that history conclusively demonstrates that the language of the first section of the Fourteenth Amendment, taken as a whole, was thought by those responsible for its submission to the people, and by those who opposed its submission, sufficiently explicit to guarantee that thereafter no state could deprive its citizens of the privileges and protections of the Bill of Rights.... And my belief seems to be in accord with the views expressed by this Court, at least for the first two decades after the Fourteenth Amendment was adopted.
>
> In 1872, four years after the Amendment was adopted, the Slaughter–House cases came to this Court ... The Court was not presented in that case with the evidence which showed that the special sponsors of the Amendment in the House and Senate had expressly explained one of its principal purposes to be to change the Constitution as construed in Barron v. Baltimore, supra, and make the Bill of Rights applicable to the states.... The Court did not meet the question of whether the safeguards of the Bill of Rights were protected against state invasion by the Fourteenth Amendment. And it specifically did not say as the Court now does, that particular provisions of the Bill of Rights could be breached by states in part, but not breached in other respects, according to this Court's notions of "civilized standards," "canons of decency," and "fundamental justice."

The partner mentions that a good bit of modern scholarship supports Justice Black's view.

The second question that the partner has asked you to consider is how to argue the case as a matter of selective incorporation. That requires the analysis of the material in your casebook on selective incorporation, most likely including cases like *Duncan v. Louisiana,* 391 U.S. 145 (1968). Unless your professor assigns *Heller,* there is no need to read the decision. But you will find the following excerpts from Justice Scalia's majority opinion helpful in preparing your *Duncan* analysis:

> Between the Restoration and the Glorious Revolution, the Stuart Kings Charles II and James II succeeded in using select militias loyal to them to suppress political dissidents, in part by disarming their opponents.... Under the auspices of the 1671 Game Act, for example, the Catholic James II had ordered general disarmaments of regions home to his Protestant enemies.... These experiences caused Englishmen to be extremely wary of concentrated military forces run by the state and to be jealous of

their arms. They accordingly obtained an assurance from William and Mary, in the Declaration of Right (which was codified as the English Bill of Rights), that Protestants would never be disarmed: "That the subjects which are Protestants may have arms for their defense suitable to their conditions and as allowed by law." ... This right has long been understood to be the predecessor to our Second Amendment.

By the time of the founding, the right to have arms had become fundamental for English subjects.... [Blackstone's] description of it cannot possibly be thought to tie it to militia or military service. It was, he said, "the natural right of resistance and self-preservation," ... and "the right of having and using arms for self-preservation and defence," ... Thus, the right secured in 1689 as a result of the Stuarts' abuses was by the time of the founding understood to be an individual right protecting against both public and private violence.

And, of course, what the Stuarts had tried to do to their political enemies, George III had tried to do to the colonists. In the tumultuous decades of the 1760's and 1770's, the Crown began to disarm the inhabitants of the most rebellious areas. That provoked polemical reactions by Americans invoking their rights as Englishmen to keep arms. A New York article of April 1769 said that "[i]t is a natural right which the people have reserved to themselves, confirmed by the Bill of Rights, to keep arms for their own defence." ...

Our interpretation is confirmed by analogous arms-bearing rights in state constitutions that preceded and immediately followed adoption of the Second Amendment. [Several] States adopted analogues to the Federal Second Amendment in the period between independence and the ratification of the Bill of Rights.

Justice Scalia's opinion is exhaustive and the quotations immediately above provide only a glimpse of his historical discussion of the English and early American history of the right to bear arms. But this should be sufficient for purposes of this simulation exercise.

Your job is to advise the senior partner on how the partner should argue the case before the Supreme Court. This requires both practical and legal considerations. For example, would an argument based on the privileges and immunities clause be legally sound? What about the practical implications of such an argument? What about the necessity of prevailing on that argument if the goal is to advance your client's interests?

CHAPTER TWO

TECHNOLOGY, SEARCHES AND WARRANTS

I. INTRODUCTION

This chapter gives you an opportunity to explore the rules governing an increasingly important area of Fourth Amendment law along with some traditional issues surrounding probable cause and warrants. The first issue in the simulation focuses on a recurrent question: is the use of technology a search within the meaning of the Fourth Amendment? The second issue focuses on the law governing the application for a search warrant. The third issue focuses on the law governing the execution of a search warrant.

This chapter consists of a brief overview of the law governing the issues described above, the defendant's motion to suppress evidence, a short memorandum in support of that motion, the search warrant and return on the warrant, and a transcript of a hearing on the defendant's motion to suppress.

II. OVERVIEW OF THE LAW

A. The Use of Technology

After material on the exclusionary rule, most of the leading Criminal Procedure casebooks begin the treatment of the Fourth Amendment with *Katz v. United States*, 389 U.S. 347 (1967). *Katz* is important for many reasons. But for purposes of this discussion, it sets out the modern definition of the term "search." It did so in a case involving modern (or relatively modern) technology.

In *Olmstead v. United States,* 277 U.S. 438 (1928),[1] a case famous for Justice Brandeis's dissenting opinion, the Court held the Fourth Amendment applied only to tangible things, not to wiretapping, and absent a trespass, the police did not violate the Fourth Amendment. By 1967, when the Court decided *Katz,* the Court had recognized that the Fourth Amendment protected conversations under some circumstances, but it retained the requirement that absent at least a technical trespass, the conduct did not amount to a search. *Compare Silverman v. United States,* 365 U.S. 505 (1961) *with Goldman v.*

---

1. Roy Olmstead was an extremely popular and successful bootlegger in Seattle at the time of the wiretap. For more interesting facts about prohibition and Roy Olmstead, see Daniel Okrent, *Last Call: The Rise and Fall of Prohibition* (2010).

United States, 316 U.S. 129 (1942). No doubt in reliance on that distinction, the F.B.I. agents investigating Katz's gambling activity attached a listening device to the outside of a phone booth that Katz regularly used.

Despite the way in which counsel framed the issue,[2] (in terms of constitutionally protected areas), the Court rejected that formulation in *Katz.* Instead, Justice Stewart's majority opinion rejected the use of concepts of trespass as controlling. The Court concluded the government action "violated the privacy upon which [Katz] justifiably relied while using the telephone booth and thus constituted a 'search and seizure' within the meaning of the Fourth Amendment." Concurring, Justice Harlan identified two distinct questions implicit in the majority's formulation of the issue: does the defendant have a subjective expectation of privacy; and if so, is it one that society is ready to recognize as reasonable? Four years later, as he was about to retire, Justice Harlan questioned his own formulation of the issue in *United States v. White,* 401 U.S. 745 (1971) (Harlan, J. dissenting). Despite that, the Court has adopted his *Katz's* concurring opinion as the correct formulation of the issue.

Justice Harlan's two-pronged test leaves much to be desired. One area where that is evident is in the case law dealing with the use of technology. Here is a sampling of the post-*Katz* case law involving technology. In *Smith v. Maryland,* 442 U.S. 735 (1979), the Court found the use of a pen register to monitor phone numbers dialed from the defendant's home phone was not a search. In *United States v. Knotts,* 460 U.S. 276 (1983), the Court found the police did not conduct a Fourth Amendment search when agents used a beeper to follow the defendant's movements on public roadways. According to the majority, "[n]othing in the Fourth Amendment prohibited the police from augmenting the sensory faculties bestowed upon them at birth with such enhancement as science and technology afforded them in this case." But if the police learn about activities that take place in the home by monitoring signals from a beeper, the police have conducted a search. *United States v. Karo,* 468 U.S. 705 (1984). In *Kyllo v. United States,* 533 U.S. 27 (2001), the police used a thermal-imaging device to detect the amount of heat emanating from the defendant's home to develop probable cause that the defendant was growing marijuana. The Court found the use of the heat-sensing device was a search. A closely divided Court found the *Karo* line of cases controlling: the use of technology was a search because it revealed information about activity within the home.

Justice Scalia compounded the difficulties with the *Katz* test in his *Kyllo* majority. There he wrote that the use of sense-enhancing technology is a search when the police gain "any information regarding the interior of the home that could not otherwise have been obtained without physical 'intrusion into a constitutionally protected area' ... *at least where ... the technology in question is not in general public use.*" (Emphasis added.) The latter language has created a bit of a stir: as pointed out by the dissent in *Kyllo,* in the interim

---

2. Counsel for Katz apparently did argue for a new legal standard during oral argument. He explains his strategy in Harvey A. Schneider, *Katz v. United States: The Untold Story,* 40 McGeorge L. Rev. 13 (2009).

between the use of the thermal-imager and the Court's decision, such devices had become widely available.[3] The concern, of course, is that *Kyllo's* test erodes our privacy as technology evolves.

Lower courts have devolved *Kyllo's* test into two questions: does the device reveal details of the interior of the home that are otherwise not available to outsiders? And is the device in general public use? For purposes of this simulation, your professor may assign you cases where these related questions have arisen or may have you argue the legal question by analogy to existing Supreme Court precedent.

As you will learn below, in this simulation, the police have used a Startron night vision instrument to look into the defendant's apartment. The following sites have some interesting information about such devices:

http://www.amazon.com/s/ref=nb_ sb_ noss?url=search-alias%3Daps&field -keywords=startron+night+vision&rh=i%3Aaps'k%3Astartron+night+vision &ajr=0

http://www.torontosurplus.com/

http://www.bookrags.com/research/night-vision-devices-woi/

During the 2011 Term, the Court decided another important technology case. In *United States v. Jones*, 565 U.S. ___ (2012), the Court found that the government violated the defendant's Fourth Amendment rights when it attached a GPS tracking device to his car and followed his movements for 28 days. While all nine justices found a Fourth Amendment violation, their reasoning differed. Justice Scalia wrote for five justices. He found that the physical intrusion on an "effect" of the defendant to obtain information amounted to a search. In part, the majority relied on the original understanding of the Fourth Amendment to reach its conclusion. As a result, the Court did not reach the government's contention that the defendant lacked a reasonable expectation of privacy because he voluntarily appeared in public. While she joined Justice Scalia's opinion, Justice Sotomayor indicated her view, similar to Justice Alito's concurring opinion, that the use of a GPS tracking device is so much more intrusive than earlier technology (like the beeper used in *Knotts*). Counting Justice Sotomayor's vote along with the justices joining Justice Alito's concurring opinion, at least five justices appear prepared to hold that long term use of a GPS device does amount to a Fourth Amendment search. *Jones* suggests the Court's willingness to rethink its technology case law in light of increasingly sophisticated devices currently in wide use.

B. The Search Warrant

If the police discover information via technology that does not amount to a search, the police should be able to rely on that information in procuring a warrant. If the use of technology is a search and the police did not have authorization (typically, probable cause and a search warrant), the police should not be able to rely on that information in procuring a warrant after the initial use of technology. As a result, where the police have used illegally

---

3. A Google search of the term "thermal imager" will come up with thousands of results. By 2011, one could buy a unit on Amazon for less than $1600.

obtained information to get a warrant, the reviewing judge should determine whether the warrant states probable cause without the illegally obtained information.

According to the Court, probable cause exists when all of circumstances within an officer's knowledge warrant a person of reasonable caution in the belief that a specifically described item subject to seizure will be found in the place to be searched. *Brinegar v. United States,* 338 U.S. 160 (1949). The standard is objective. A judge reviewing a warrant should not credit "bald and unilluminating" assertions; that is, the affiant must explain the basis of the affiant's belief.

The Court has stated that the probable cause standard is a practical, common sense judgment. Further, in *United States v. Leon* 468 U.S. 897 (1984), the Court held that "the Fourth Amendment exclusionary rule should be modified so as not to bar the use in the prosecution's case-in-chief of evidence obtained by officers acting in reasonable reliance on a search warrant issued by a detached and neutral magistrate but ultimately found to be unsupported by probable cause." Reliance on the issuance of a warrant has its limits, as *Leon* made clear. For example, an officer may not rely "on a warrant based on an affidavit 'so lacking in indicia of probable cause as to render official belief in its existence entirely unreasonable.'" Also, an officer may not rely on a warrant that is "so facially deficient—i.e., in failing to particularize the place to be searched or things to be seized—that the executing officers cannot reasonably presume it to be valid." More recently, the Court has suggested that the exclusionary rule does not apply absent a showing that the police conduct amounted to more than "isolated" "nonrecurring" negligence. *Herring v. United States,* 555 U.S. 135 (2009). *Davis v. United States,* 131 S.Ct. 2419 (2011) provides further evidence that the Court is in the process of reshaping the exclusionary rule.

Other issues arise when the police execute a warrant. A warrant must state with particularity the place to be searched and the things to be seized. Under the authorization of the warrant, the police may search the entire area covered by the warrant's description. But the police must limit the scope of the search to areas where the items described in the warrant may be located. The police exceed their authority if they look into areas where the items identified in the search warrant could not be located. If the police are looking in such an area and come upon evidence not listed in the warrant, the police may seize the item as long as it meets the requirements of the plain view doctrine: the police must be lawfully present where they are looking and they must have probable cause of the item's evidentiary value.

III. PEOPLE v. EDWIN MULLET

In the
SUPERIOR COURT
FOR THE COUNTY OF McGEORGE

State of Pacific
Plaintiff

Criminal Action No. 00–568–JD

vs.

Judge: Michael Vitiello

Defendant Edwin Mullet

I. Defendant's Motion to Suppress

Defendant, being a person aggrieved by an unlawful search and seizure, moves to suppress for use as evidence all items obtained by said search and seizure and all other evidence obtained as a result thereof on the following grounds:

1. On August 15, YR–02, the police received a report of an armed robbery at the McGeorge City Art Museum in McGeorge City. One of the two robbers beat one of the docents, leaving him in critical condition.

2. Thereafter, the police learned the two robbers got away with three valuable works of local artist Ronald Peters, each valued at more than $100,000.

3. The police made no progress in locating the robbers for more than three months.

4. In late November, police received an anonymous tip that indicated Tony Basso was one of the robbers.

5. On December 1, YR–02, police attempted to question Basso, but Basso died of wounds received in a shootout with police.

6. Convinced that Basso's friend Edwin Mullet was involved in the robbery, the police set up surveillance of Mr. Mullet's apartment at 169 Fifth Avenue, McGeorge City. To learn whether Mr. Mullet had the paintings in his apartment, the police gained access to an apartment on the third floor of a building across the street from Mr. Mullet's.

7. The police used a Startron night vision device to peer into Mr. Mullet's apartment.

8. After prolonged surveillance, the police finally spotted one of the works of art in Mr. Mullet's apartment on March 27, YR–01.

9. Based on that observation, the police secured a search warrant of Mr. Mullet's apartment on March 29, YR–01. In the course of the search, the police discovered two of the works of art taken from the museum. In addition,

the police seized several items, including a 9mm pistol found in a drawer in Mr. Mullet's bedroom and several ordinary tools.

10. The use of the Startron night vision device was a search conducted by the police without probable cause and a warrant. Therefore, use of the information learned through that search should not have been included in the search warrant.

11. Without the illegally obtained evidence, the warrant lacked sufficient information to create probable cause. Therefore, all evidence seized pursuant to the warrant must be suppressed.

12. Even if the warrant was sufficient, the police exceeded the scope of the warrant when they found Mr. Mullet's handgun. Therefore, the weapon should be suppressed.

13. The seizure of Mr. Mullet's tools was illegal because the police lacked probable cause to believe they had evidentiary value. Therefore, the Mr. Mullet's tools should be suppressed.

Dated: September 6, YR–01

Respectfully submitted,

Carl Russell

Carl Russell
Attorney-at-Law
16 Napa Road
McGeorge City, Pacific 95817
Telephone: (797) 555–5100
Attorney for Defendant

In the
SUPERIOR COURT
FOR THE COUNTY OF McGEORGE

State of Pacific
Plaintiff

00–568–JD

vs.

Judge: Michael Vitiello

Defendant Edwin Mullet

Memorandum of Points and Authorities on Behalf of Defendant

I. Introduction

Edwin Mullet has been charged with two counts of violating Pacific Penal Code § 211 (armed robbery), one count of § 245 (aggravated assault), and three counts of § 287 (grand theft), all arising out of the August 15, YR–02 robbery at the McGeorge City Art Museum.

II. Facts

On August 15, YR–02, the McGeorge City Police Department received a 911 call that two armed men had stolen three paintings from the McGeorge City Art Museum. With limited information about the identity of the robbers, the police investigation stalled. Months into their investigation, the police received an anonymous tip that Tony Basso was one of the robbers. While trying to question Basso, the police ended up in a shootout, resulting in Basso's death. The police received no information from Basso.

Solely based on rumors that Basso was friends with Mr. Mullet, the police began a prolonged and extensive surveillance of his apartment. The police rented an apartment on the third floor of a building across the street from Mr. Mullet. The police set up 24/7 surveillance to see whether Mr. Mullet had proceeds of the robbery. Over many weeks, the police collected no incriminating evidence to link the defendant to the robbery. Finally, by using a Startron night vision device, the police were able to view into Mr. Mullet's apartment at night through a partially raised window covering. An officer observed what the officer believed was one of the paintings taken in the robbery.

Using that information, an officer from the McGeorge Police Department procured a search warrant on March 29, YR–01. That warrant necessarily relied on the information gathered through their prolonged search of Mr. Mullet's apartment.

While executing that warrant, the police not only looked where they might find a painting but also searched Mr. Mullet's bedroom drawer. There, an officer found a 9 mm pistol. Further, an officer found several hand tools in a closet in Mr. Mullet's kitchen.

On April 20, YR–01, a grand jury indicted Mr. Mullet on two counts of armed robbery, one count of aggravated assault, and three counts of grand theft.

III. Argument

Mr. Mullet had a right to be free from unreasonable searches and seizures. By using a Startron night vision device, the police conducted a search. That search was illegal because the police lacked probable cause to believe that evidence of the crime under investigation would be found in Mr. Mullet's apartment. Further, because the police relied on their observations, use of that information in procuring a search warrant for Mr. Mullet's apartment renders the warrant illegal because, without the results of the illegal search, the warrant did not state adequate probable cause to believe Mr. Mullet's apartment contained evidence of a crime.

Alternatively, the police exceeded the scope of the warrant when they looked in Mr. Mullet's bedroom drawer where they found a handgun. In addition, the police lacked any justification for the seizure of ordinary hand tools from Mr. Mullet's premises.

IV. Conclusion

For the foregoing reasons, Mr. Mullet requests the court to suppress all of the evidence obtained as a result of the violation of his Fourth Amendment rights.

Respectfully submitted,

Carl Russell

Carl Russell

Attorney-at-Law
16 Napa Rd.
McGeorge City, Pacific 95817
Telephone: (797) 555–5100

IV. THE SEARCH WARRANT

Search Warrant 13 YR–01

STATE OF PACIFIC—COUNTY OF MCGEORGE

SEARCH WARRANT AND AFFIDAVIT
(AFFIDAVIT)

    ___J a m e s   F i s h___ swears under oath that the facts expressed by
(Name of Affiant)
him/her in this Search Warrant and Affidavit and in the attached and incorporated statement of probable cause are true and that based thereon he/she has probable cause to believe and does believe that the property. and/or person described below is lawfully seizable pursuant to Pacific Penal Code Section 1524, as indicated below, and is now located at the locations set forth below. Wherefore, affiant requests that this Search Warrant be issued.

_____*James Fish*_____,
(Signature of Affiant)

NIGHT SEARCH REQUESTED: NO

(SEARCH WARRANT)

THE PEOPLE OF THE STATE OF PACIFIC TO ANY PEACE OFFICER IN THE COUNTY OF MCGEORGE:

Proof by affidavit having been made before me by ____J a m e s   F i s h____
(Name of Affiant)
that there is probable cause to believe that the property and/or Person described herein may he found at the locations set forth herein and is lawfully seizable pursuant to Pacific Penal Code Section 1524 as indicated below by "x"(s) in that:

_X_ it was stolen or embezzled

____ it was used as the means of committing a felony

____ it is possessed by a person with the intent to use it as a means of committing a public offense or is possessed by another to whom he or she may have delivered it for the purpose of concealing it or preventing its discovery,

____ it tends to show that a felony has been committed or that a particular person has committed a felony,

____ it tends to show that sexual exploitation of a child in violation of Section 311.3, or depiction of sexual conduct of a person under the age of 18 years, in violation of Section 311.11, has occurred or is occurring

____ there is a warrant for the person's arrest.

YOU ARE THEREFORE COMMANDED TO SEARCH:

See attached and incorporated description page.

FOR FOLLOWING PROPERTY/PERSON:

See attached and incorporated description page.

AND TO SEIZE IT IF FOUND and bring it forthwith before me, or this court, at the courthouse of this court. This Search Warrant and incorporated Affidavit was sworn to as true and subscribed before me this ___29th___ day of ___March___, YR–01, ___10:15___ **A.M.** Wherefore, I find probable cause for the issuance of this Search Warrant and do issue it.

___*Jeremy Taylor*___,
   (Signature of Magistrate)

NIGHT SEARCH REQUESTED: NO

Judge of the Superior Court, ___Jeremy Taylor, Judge___
Judicial District, City and County of McGeorge

YOU ARE THEREFORE COMMANDED TO SEARCH:

The premises at: 169 Fifth Avenue, McGeorge City, Apartment 3 F.

THE FOLLOWING VEHICLE:
AND THE FOLLOWING PERSONS: Edwin Mullet

FOR THE FOLLOWING PROPERTY: a painting by Ronald Peters entitled "Snow in August," a painting by Ronald Peters entitled "A Dancing Maiden; and a painting by Ronald Peter entitled 'Night in Davis.' "

STATEMENT OF PROBABLE CAUSE

On August 15, YR–02, the McGeorge City Police Department received a 911 call of a robbery in progress at the McGeorge City Art Museum. Responding Officers Albert Capone and Roy Olmstead learned that two armed and masked men had badly beaten a docent, threatened the docent and a Museum security guard, and stolen three highly valuable paintings by Pacific artist Ronald Peters. Those paintings are listed above.

On November 20, YR–02, Olmstead received an anonymous phone call from a person who demonstrated a great deal of familiarity with the facts surrounding the robbery of the art museum, including the method of planning and operation of the robbery. For example, the informant explained that they intended to enter at the end of the day when no patrons would be there and the security force would be limited to one or two employees. Further, the informant stated Tony Basso was one of the robbers. The informant did not know the other robber's name but described him in some detail.

In an effort to confirm that tip, Officer Capone attempted to interview Basso on December 1, YR–02. Basso refused to cooperate and pulled a weapon on the officer, which resulted in a shootout and led to Basso's death from a gunshot wound. Specifically, Officer Capone told Basso before the shootout that the police were investigating his and his gang's involvement in the museum robbery.

Because affiant knew that Edwin Mullet was a criminal associate of Tony Basso, and because both men fit the descriptions of the robbers, affiant set up surveillance of Mullet's apartment at 169 Fifth Avenue in McGeorge City. To better view the apartment, affiant secured cooperation from landlord Jim Corso, owner of 156 Fifth Avenue. Corso allowed McGeorge City Police officers to use a third floor apartment to set up surveillance of Mullet's apartment. To enhance our sense of sight, affiant secured a Startron Night Vision Scope and placed it in the apartment for officers assigned to surveillance.

On several occasions during the period of surveillance, affiant saw known associates of Tony Basso enter Mullet's apartment building. On three occasions, said affiant witnessed said associates confer with Mullet in the front of 169 Fifth Avenue. Further, during the period of time, affiant was able to confirm that Mullet has no visible means of support.

On March 27 of YR–01, affiant was able to see into Mullet's apartment and watched him unroll what affiant knew to be "Dancing Maiden," one of the three paintings stolen in August 15 armed robbery.

Continued surveillance of Mullet's apartment has led affiant to believe the painting is still located in Mullet's apartment at 169 Fifth Avenue in McGeorge City. Wherefore, your affiant requests a warrant to issue to search said apartment.

The affiant's opinion is based upon his experience and training as an officer and the facts set forth in this affidavit.

SW NO. 13, YR–01

STATE OF PACIFIC—COUNTY OF MCGEORGE

RETURN TO SEARCH WARRANT

  J a m e s   F i s h,   being sworn, says that he/she conducted a search pursu-
  (Name of Affiant)
ant to the below described search warrant:

Issuing Magistrate: Jeremy Taylor   ,

Magistrate's Court: Superior Court, Judicial District City and County of McGeorge

Date of Issuance: March 29, YR–01   ,

Date of Service: March 29, YR–01   ,
and searched the following location(s), vehicle(s), and person(s):

Apartment 3F, 169 Fifth Avenue, McGeorge City, Pacific.

And seized the items*

____ described in the attached and incorporated inventory.

 X described below:

One painting, Dancing Maiden by Ronald Peters

One 9 millimeter Walther P99 German semi-automatic pistol

Set of six flat head screwdrivers

One six-piece BROCKAGE locksmith kit

I further swear that this is a true and detailed account of all the property taken by me pursuant to the search warrant and that pursuant to Pacific Penal Code Sections 1528 and 1536 this property will be retained in my custody, subject to the order of this court or of any other court in which the offense in respect to which the seized property is triable.

_____*James Fish*_____ ,
   (Signature of Affiant)

Sworn to and subscribed before me this ___29th___ day of ___March YR–01___

_____*Jeremy Taylor*_____ ,
   (Signature of Magistrate)

Judge of the Superior Court, Judicial District City and County of McGeorge

*List **all** items seized, including those not specifically listed on the warrant.

V. PEOPLE v. MULLET: THE HEARING ON THE MOTION

Transcript of the hearing on Defendant
Edwin Mullet's Motion to Suppress

Wednesday, January 6, YR–00

The matter of People of the State of Pacific v. Defendant Edwin Mullet, case number 00–568–JD, came before the Honorable Michael Vitiello, Judge of the Superior Court of Pacific, County of McGeorge.

THE COURT: Good afternoon, ladies and gentlemen. Okay. For the record, this is People of the State of Pacific v. Wade Kirby.

MR. RUSSELL: No, Your Honor. This is People v. Edwin Mullet. The Wade hearing is later this week, I believe.

THE COURT: Oh, thank you for clearing that up. Okay, Mr. Russell, Ms. Connell, enter your appearances for the record.

MS. CONNELL: Alicia Connell for the People of Pacific.

MR. RUSSELL: Carl Russell for Mr. Mullet.

THE COURT: Now I remember this case. The procedure is, well, we need to discuss the order that you are going to be arguing. Mr. Russell, are you attacking the sufficiency of the warrant?

MR. RUSSELL: In part, Your Honor. Mr. Mullet has challenged the police conduct in using a night vision instrument to search his apartment. If you find that conduct to be a search, as I think you must under the prevailing case law, then we get to the warrant question. There is also a scope of the warrant concern, Your Honor.

THE COURT: Okay. Thanks for the clarification. So Ms. Connell, you agree that you carry the initial burden of going forward on the search question, now that Mr. Russell has put it in issue?

MS. CONNELL: Yes, Your Honor, that is certainly my understanding.

THE COURT: Well then, let's get going. Ms. Connell would you call your first witness or do we have more preliminary matters to get out of the way?

MS. CONNELL: Nothing else, Your Honor. The People call Officer James Fish.

Officer James Fish was called as a witness, being duly sworn, was examined and testified as follows:

DIRECT EXAMINATION

MS. CONNELL: Officer, would you please state your name for the court and spell your name for the court reporter?

A. James Fish. J–A–M–E–S; F–I–S–H.

Q. And would you tell the court your background with the McGeorge City Police Department?

1　　　A. Sure. I graduated from the McGeorge Police Academy in YR–08.
2　I went into the Army and did two years of service after I graduated from
3　the academy. I have been on the force here in McGeorge since I got my
4　honorable discharge from the service.

5　　　Q. Okay. Take us back to August, YR–02, around August 15. Were
6　you involved in investigating an armed robbery?

7　　　A. Actually, I was involved in several investigations. But I assume
8　that you mean the robbery at the Museum.

9　　　Q. I do mean that robbery.

10　　　A. Well, I was not part of the response team that went to the crime
11　scene on August 15. But I took statements from one of the victims a
12　couple of days later. I interviewed John Christopher. He is an elderly
13　man, working as a guide or a, you know.

14　　　Q. A docent?

15　　　A. Yeah. He took a pretty bad beating from one of the robbers.

16　　　Q. Was he able to give you a description of the robbers?

17　　　A. He gave me some useful information.

18　　　Q. Anything in particular?

19　　　A. Yes. The robbers wore masks but he described their physiques.
20　Both were big men, big chests, and big hands.

21　　　Q. Any other identifying features?

22　　　MR. RUSSELL: Your Honor, I hesitate to object, but I am not quite
23　sure where this line of questioning is going. I know how Your Honor likes
24　us to stay on point so I wonder, like I said, where we are going.

25　　　THE COURT: Ms. Connell, any light on the matter?

26　　　MS. CONNELL: Yes, Your Honor. I am getting some background
27　before we go to the complained of conduct. And this information will be
28　relevant to the probable cause question when we get to the warrant dis-
29　cussion.

30　　　THE COURT: Mr. Russell, does that clear up the point?

31　　　MR. RUSSELL: No, Your Honor. The officer seems to be testifying
32　about facts outside the four corners of the warrant. If so, those facts are
33　not relevant to the probable cause issue.

34　　　THE COURT: Ms. Connell, Mr. Russell has a point. Any response to
35　his argument before I rule?

36　　　MS. CONNELL: It helps explain the background; it helps set the
37　stage for what the officer did next.

38　　　THE COURT: Alright. Keep it brief.

39　　　MS. CONNELL: Thank you, Your Honor. Officer Fish, so you took a
40　description from the victim. Did he include any other information of rel-
41　evance?

42　　　A. Well, he described a brutal beating. It was unprovoked; the guys
43　who did it were bad operators.

1   Q.   Anything else that you learned at the time?

2   A.   Nothing comes to mind. But I was not assigned to the case—I
3 asked to be.

4   Q.   Okay. So you got assigned to the case, and what happened to the
5 investigation?

6   A.   Officer Olmstead got a tip from a CI.

7   MR. RUSSELL: Objection, pure hearsay.

8   THE COURT: It looks pretty pure to me too. Sustained. Ms. Connell,
9 you will have Officer Olmstead on the stand for that purpose, to get at
10 what he heard?

11   MS. CONNELL: Yes, Your Honor. Back to you, Officer Fish; what
12 happened next in your investigation that you can testify to doing or learn-
13 ing yourself?

14   A.   Well, let's see. After the shootout with Tony Basso, I decided that
15 we should take a look at the defendant.

16   THE COURT: Let me stop you for a second. Ms. Connell, I read the
17 papers and know about the shoot out. But there is nothing in the record
18 about it. I guess you are trying to avoid the hearsay problem. Mr. Russell,
19 before we get into objections and counterarguments, I am going to let Ms.
20 Connell get to the heart of the matter. Officer, tell us about the shootout.

21   A.   Sure. Based on the tip that I was telling or trying to tell you
22 about, Ms. Connell, Officers Capone and Olmstead tried to interview Tony
23 Basso. He was a known criminal with a long record of violent crime. He
24 also was a big man, with a big chest, and a big gut. Rather than talking
25 to the officers, though, he decided to fight his way out of a jam.

26   Q.   After you learned about Basso's involvement ...

27   MR. RUSSELL: Objection. There is no evidence that Tony Basso was
28 involved in the crime, other than an uncorroborated tip.

29   THE COURT: Can you link it up, Ms. Connell?

30   MS. CONNELL: Your Honor, with a little leeway, we already have a
31 tip and then, at least when we get Officer Olmstead on the stand, you will
32 hear that he and his partner told Basso what they were investigating.
33 That creates a strong inference of his involvement. If he had nothing to
34 do with the robbery, why would he start shooting at the officers?

35   THE COURT: Okay. I am not going to tell you how to present your
36 case, Ms. Connell. But I would like to hear the evidence on the first issue
37 that Mr. Russell has raised, whether the use of technology was a search.

38   MS. CONNELL: Thank you for your forbearance, Your Honor. I will
39 get right there. Officer Fish, so after Tony Basso resisted arrest and got
40 shot, you focused on the defendant as a prime suspect in the crime
41 because he was Basso's criminal associate, didn't you?

42   MR. RUSSELL: Again, with deference, Your Honor, I don't like to
43 object on technical grounds, but apart from leading the witness and tes-
44 tifying herself, there is no evidence that Mr. Mullet was a criminal asso-
45 ciate of Tony Basso's.

1   THE COURT: Sustained.

2   MS. CONNELL: Officer, did you focus on the defendant as a suspect
3   after the shootout?

4   A. I did.

5   Q. Why?

6   A. Not only was Mullet reputed to be a Basso associate, but also I
7   arrested the defendant and Basso in YR–03.

8   Q. What for?

9   A. Prostitution.

10   Q. You don't mean that they were prostitutes?

11   A. No. But they ran a prostitution ring together.

12   Q. Other than that fact, do you have any idea of why Mullet had the
13   reputation for being a Basso associate?

14   A. Check out their rap sheets. I see that Mr. Russell is on his feet.
15   Should I continue?

16   THE COURT: Officer, you can continue unless an attorney says the
17   magic word.

18   MR. RUSSELL: I object.

19   THE COURT: Do you dispute that their rap sheets show that they
20   were arrested together on other occasions? Everyone in this courthouse
21   knows about Basso and Mullet. I am sure that Ms. Connell can bring in
22   their records.

23   MR. RUSSELL: I withdraw the objection.

24   MS. CONNELL: Officer, so why else did you believe that the defen-
25   dant was a Basso associate?

26   A. We often set up surveillance in Basso's neighborhood, to check
27   out who hung out with who.

28   Q. And what did you learn from those observations?

29   A. They spent a lot of time together.

30   Q. After you learned about Basso's involvement in the robbery and
31   art theft, what did you do?

32   A. We started to watch the defendant.

33   Q. Did you call him in for questioning?

34   A. No.

35   Q. Why not?

36   A. We did not want to have another shootout. And we did not want
37   to let the defendant know that we suspected him. We didn't want him to
38   try to get rid of the paintings.

39   Q. So you set up a surveillance of the defendant's apartment, you
40   said?

41   A. We did.

1   Q. Where did you set it up?

2   A. The landlord of the building across the street from the defen-
3   dant's place is an honest guy. He let us use an empty third floor apart-
4   ment across from the defendant's.

5   Q. Were you able to see what went on in the defendant's apartment?

6   A. From time to time we did. Sometimes, he had the lights on and
7   the shades up; during the day, we could see right into his apartment. And
8   there was a street lamp near his window; it shined a lot of light in the
9   area.

10   Q. You eventually saw that the defendant had one of the paintings
11   in his apartment, didn't you?

12   A. I did.

13   Q. How did you get that particular viewing?

14   A. I requisitioned a Startron, a Starlight scope from the depart-
15   ment.

16   Q. Would you describe this instrument?

17   A. The full name of this item is Night Vision Sight, Individual
18   Served Weapon, AN/PVS–4. Night vision technology allows vision at
19   night. It has been around since the 1950s, but really with the first Gulf
20   War, the technology really came on line. This particular unit that I used
21   was developed in the 1970's, back when we were still in Vietnam. More
22   recently, there is even a newer generation. But we still work with the ones
23   that we have had for several years. They are less expensive and pretty
24   easy to get hold of.

25   Q. How does this kind of equipment work?

26   MR. RUSSELL: Objection. Ms. Connell has not qualified him as an
27   expert on this device.

28   THE COURT: Ms. Connell, go ahead and qualify him.

29   MS. CONNELL: Do you have any experience with night vision
30   devices?

31   A. I do. When I was in the service, I was assigned to acquisitions. I
32   had to secure materiel for my unit. Among those items I had to procure
33   were night goggles and other kinds of night scopes. My army training
34   included training in the technology that I had to order.

35   Q. Did you learn about the kind of night vision instrument that you
36   used in this case?

37   A. I did. That was still available when I was in the service, even
38   though it was being phased out.

39   Q. So tell us about the instrument that you used in this case.

40   A. Because of its use of an electrostatic inverter, this device is suit-
41   able for night conditions, even without starlight.

42   Q. So what did you see in the defendant's apartment on March 27?

43   A. I saw him come into the room, open a closet and take out a large
44   cardboard tube.

1 Q. And why did you think that was the painting taken in the
2 August 15 armed robbery?

3 A. He opened the tube and unrolled the painting.

4 Q. You could tell that it was the Dancing Maiden painting?

5 A. Yes.

6 Q. How could you tell?

7 A. The defendant unrolled it and placed it on a sofa where I could
8 see it pretty clearly.

9 Q. What did you do next?

10 A. After I saw the painting, two days later, I swore out a search
11 warrant. We kept surveillance on the apartment hoping the defendant did
12 not try to run with the painting.

13 MS. CONNELL: Your Honor, at this point, I am done with Officer
14 Fish as far as the discovery of the painting goes. Would it be best to con-
15 tinue and discuss with him his role in finding evidence when he executed
16 the warrant?

17 THE COURT: Ms. Connell, it is your case to try, but why don't you
18 just go ahead and finish up with the direct evidence? Let's get all of the
19 evidence in the record before we end the hearing.

20 MS. CONNELL: Okay. Officer Fish, so did you execute the search
21 warrant that was issued for a search of the defendant's apartment?

22 A. I did.

23 Q. Would you describe what happened when you arrived at the
24 apartment?

25 A. Sure. I was there with backup, this time it was Olmstead and
26 Capone, as well. I knocked and announced at the front door of the apart-
27 ment. Two other officers were stationed at the back of the house to be sure
28 that the defendant did not try to leave. Olmstead and Capone was with
29 me in the hallway.

30 Q. They were? Did the defendant come to the door?

31 A. He did.

32 Q. Did he open the door or did you have to force it open?

33 A. No, he was cooperative.

34 Q. Once you entered, how did you proceed?

35 A. I told the defendant that we were here to execute the warrant,
36 and I showed him the warrant. Meanwhile, Olmstead drew his weapon
37 and did a quick sweep through the apartment to be sure that no one else
38 was there. Capone told the defendant that he had to be handcuffed dur-
39 ing the search. The defendant was all cooperative.

40 Q. How many rooms are in the apartment?

41 A. It is a two bedroom, so I guess four rooms.

42 Q. And then, after you knocked and entered and had the defendant
43 cuffed, what did you do?

1   A. Well, Capone stayed with the defendant to keep an eye on him.
2   Olmstead went into the back bedroom. I went into the master bedroom; I
3   looked quickly into a dressing table next to the bed. That is where guys
4   often keep weapons. And bingo, I found a nine millimeter.

5   Q. Where did you find the painting?

6   A. I searched the bedroom pretty quickly and then came into the
7   living room and found the cardboard tube in the closet near the sofa. I
8   opened it and saw what I knew was the painting.

9   Q. Alright. And the tools?

10   A. I did not find them.

11   Q. Who did?

12   A. Roy. I mean Officer Olmstead.

13   MS. CONNELL: That is all I have, Your Honor.

14   <center>CROSS EXAMINATION</center>

15   MR. RUSSELL: Officer, how are you doing today?

16   A. I am fine, Mr. Russell.

17   Q. I am glad to hear that. I would like to go back to the surveillance
18   of the defendant's apartment. I don't think that the warrant stated when
19   the surveillance began. Can you tell me when it began?

20   A. It was in early January, last year.

21   Q. And you said that the surveillance was 24/7, didn't you?

22   A. Yes.

23   Q. So someone, often you, was watching the apartment from across
24   the street for almost three months, 24 hours a day, 7 days a week, is that
25   what you just said?

26   A. Not three months; whatever.

27   Q. Well, early January through the end of March is almost three
28   months, isn't it?

29   MS. CONNELL: Objection, argumentative.

30   THE COURT: Well, technically, you are right. And Mr. Russell, I can
31   do the math.

32   MR. RUSSELL: So, Officer Fish, during the day, you couldn't see into
33   the defendant's apartment, could you?

34   A. Sometimes.

35   Q. Why not all the time?

36   A. The defendant kept his shades drawn some of the time. But
37   sometimes, he had the shades up, and we could see in without difficulty.

38   Q. During those times, though, you never saw him take the paint-
39   ing out of the closet, did you?

40   A. No.

41   Q. And at night, over three months or almost three months, 24/7,
42   you watched the defendant's apartment by using night goggles or a night
43   vision scope, correct?

1   A. Yes.

2   Q. So, by using the night vision scope, you could see into his apart-
3 ment even with the lights out, right?

4   A. Yes.

5   Q. And, I mean, that is the point of using the night vision scope,
6 isn't it?

7   A. Yes. But we might have been able to see in because of the street
8 light nearby.

9   Q. So during about three months, 24/7, you must have seen the
10 defendant engaged in some pretty intimate activities while he had no idea
11 you were looking into his apartment, right?

12   A. Not really.

13   Q. Why not?

14   A. Well, he kept his shades or blinds closed a lot.

15   Q. So on most evenings, you did not have much of a view into his
16 apartment because the blinds were drawn, is that what you are telling
17 me?

18   A. I just told you that.

19   Q. And did you ever see into the apartment using the night vision
20 scope? Wait, let me rephrase the question. You continued to watch 24/7 for
21 almost three months but never got a view into his apartment; that makes
22 no sense to me.

23   MS. CONNELL: Objection; that is not a question. It is argumenta-
24 tive.

25   THE COURT: Sustained.

26   MR. RUSSELL: Okay, Officer Fish, let me ask again. Are you testify-
27 ing that you did not get a view into the apartment over a three or almost
28 three month period even though you and members of the department
29 watched all night long for that period of time?

30   A. No. We could see in from time to time.

31   Q. So tell us about how often you could see into the apartment and
32 what you saw.

33   A. When?

34   MR. RUSSELL: Your Honor, would you instruct the witness to
35 answer the question?

36   THE COURT: Mr. Russell, okay. The question was too open-ended,
37 but I see where we are having trouble. Officer, let me interfere for a sec-
38 ond. Other than on the night of March 27, can you estimate how often you
39 saw into the apartment at night by using the night vision scope?

40   A. Maybe a half dozen or a dozen times.

41   THE COURT: Thank you. Mr. Russell, I will leave the rest to you.

42   MR. RUSSELL: Thank you, Your Honor. Officer, tell us what you saw
43 when you could see into the apartment.

1   A.   It depended.

2   Q.   Well, the first time you saw into the apartment, what did you
3   see?

4   A.   I saw the defendant having sex with a woman on the sofa.

5   Q.   The defendant left his window wide open for all to see in?

6   A.   No.

7   Q.   Then describe how you were able to see into the apartment.

8   A.   We had the night scope trained on the window that we could see;
9   the shade was drawn but the window was cracked open and the shade
10   was pulled up a foot or so. And a breeze may have moved the window cov-
11   ering. That allowed us to see in.

12   Q.   But you could not have seen into the apartment and known what
13   was going on without the night vision device, could you?

14   A.   Maybe.

15   Q.   So you said that you saw into the apartment only a half dozen
16   times; what did you see on those occasions?

17   A.   That's not what I said. It was a dozen times, maybe.

18   Q.   My apologies, but the question stands—what did you see on
19   those occasions?

20   A.   Not much. Sitting, we saw him sitting by himself in the dark.
21   Not much else. We saw him watching television; we could see the light of
22   TV set a lot.

23   Q.   And during that time, when you could see into the apartment,
24   you did not see anything else that tied the defendant to the robbery or
25   theft, did you? I mean, you did not include anything else in the probable
26   cause section of the warrant, did you?

27   A.   I am not sure which question you want me to answer.

28   Q.   Well, you did not see anything else that tied the defendant to the
29   crimes he's charged with, did you?

30   A.   Yes, we saw him come outside and talk with Basso associates.

31   Q.   No, I mean in the apartment.

32   A.   No, nothing else, until March 27 when we saw what we needed
33   to see.

34   Q.   And from what I see in the probable cause section of the warrant,
35   the only other evidence that you learned through surveillance was that on
36   two or three occasions, Mr. Mullet talked to some of Tony Basso's friends,
37   isn't that correct?

38   A.   Basso's criminal associates.

39   Q.   How do you know that … I withdraw that question. You did not
40   see any money pass hands between the defendant and Basso's friends, did
41   you?

42   A.   No.

1   Q. Okay. So on the night of March 27, when you saw the painting or
2 what you thought was the painting, how could you determine that this
3 was the painting through a slit in the shades, or a six-inch opening in the
4 shades?

5   A. I didn't.

6   Q. What do you mean?

7   A. On the night of 27th, the shades were up more than a few inches.

8   Q. But no lights were on in the apartment, were they?

9   A. No.

10   Q. You still needed the night vision scope to see into the apartment,
11 didn't you?

12   A. Maybe.

13   Q. Do you remember if there was any outside lighting shining into
14 the apartment, a street light or moonlight? I should mention that I have
15 the weather report for that evening here.

16   A. A little light from the street light, a little moonlight.

17   Q. And that little bit of light would not have allowed you to view the
18 painting without the night device, correct?

19   A. That isn't what I just said, is it? I might have seen it without the
20 vision scope.

21   Q. Also, you saw the painting through a small opening in the win-
22 dow covering; this must be a pretty big painting for you to have recog-
23 nized it from across the street?

24   A. It is what it is.

25   Q. Well, what is it, if you can tell me how large it is?

26   A. Four feet high, six feet long.

27   Q. The cardboard tube in which it was stored must have been pretty
28 big, yes?

29   A. Depends on what you mean by pretty big, Mr. Russell.

30   Q. How long was the tube, officer?

31   A. Tall enough to hold the painting.

32   Q. So six feet tall, isn't that correct? I have a ruler if we need to
33 measure it.

34   A. I guess, six feet, about that.

35   Q. Moving on, Officer, so on March 29, you were one of the officers
36 who executed the search warrant, weren't you?

37   A. Yes.

38   Q. So, once you gained entrance into the defendant's premises, you
39 followed proper procedure and handcuffed the defendant, didn't you?

40   A. I did not put on the handcuffs, but we did follow routine proce-
41 dure.

1   Q. Then, once he was handcuffed, you said that Capone determined
2 that no one else was in the home, isn't that correct?

3   A. Pretty much so.

4   Q. And while you began to search, Olmstead stayed with the defen-
5 dant to make sure that he was not a risk to you and Capone, isn't that
6 correct?

7   A. That is correct.

8   Q. When you opened the drawer in the otherwise empty bedroom,
9 you were not looking for a large painting in the bedroom night stand,
10 were you?

11   A. No.

12   Q. One more question. I am sorry, that is it for me. I was going to
13 ask the officer about the tools but he admitted that he did not find them.

14   REDIRECT EXAMINATION

15   THE COURT: Ms. Connell, do you have any more direct examina-
16 tion?

17   MS. CONNELL: I do have one or two more questions. Officer, you
18 looked into the bedside table to be sure that the defendant did not have a
19 weapon hidden there, didn't you?

20   A. Yes.

21   Q. You knew the defendant's reputation for violence, didn't you and
22 you suspected that the defendant would be armed?

23   A. Yes, I did. I saw Mr. Christopher and knew how he'd been pistol
24 whipped by the robbers.

25   MS. CONNELL: Nothing further, Your Honor.

26   RECROSS EXAMINATION

27   MR. RUSSELL: Officer Fish, you can't point to anything that took
28 place on March 27th that led you to believe that the defendant was armed
29 or dangerous, can you?

30   A. I knew that he was one of the robbers and that he and Basso had
31 pistol-whipped an elderly gentleman, almost killed him. I knew that faced
32 with this crime, Basso had been willing to kill a police officer rather than
33 be taken into custody. I knew that this guy was mobbed up. I knew that
34 this guy is over 200 pounds and a mean SOB. But no, nothing more than
35 that. Oh, yeah, I knew that he could at any moment overpower Olmstead
36 and grab a weapon.

37   Q. Really? Olmstead, Officer Olmstead had the defendant hand-
38 cuffed in the other room, didn't he?

39   A. Yes.

40   Q. And did Olmstead have out his service revolver, surely he would
41 have done so, had he been afraid of the defendant, wouldn't he?

42   A. I guess so.

43   MR. RUSSELL: Nothing further, Your Honor.

1   THE COURT: Officer, you are excused. Folks, let's take a break. This
2 has been a long session. Reconvene in thirty minutes, and let's see where
3 we are.

4   (Recess: 2:30 PM)

5   (Court in session: 3:15 PM)

6   THE COURT: So let me see where we are. Are you ready to argue the
7 case and the sufficiency of the warrant?

8   MS. CONNELL: I have one more witness.

9   THE COURT: My apologies. I forgot that you said so earlier today.

10   Officer Roy Olmstead was called as a witness, being duly sworn, was
11 examined and testified as follows:

DIRECT EXAMINATION

13   MS. CONNELL: Officer, would you please state your name for the
14 court and spell your name for the court reporter?

15   A.   Roy Olmstead. You just need me to spell Olmstead. O–L–M–S–
16 T–E–A–D.

17   Q.   And would you tell the court your background with the
18 McGeorge City Police Department?

19   A.   Well, I went to the Pacific Police Academy in YR–05. I was hired
20 first by the Spring Garden Police Department in YR–04 and then by
21 McGeorge in YR–03.

22   Q.   Take us to the events surrounding the robbery, beating, and theft
23 at the McGeorge City Art Museum on August 15, YR–02.

24   A.   Okay. My partner and me responded to a 911 call that the rob-
25 bery had taken place. Officer Capone and I arrived at the museum right
26 after the call.

27   THE COURT: Ms. Connell, may I make a suggestion? You need this
28 officer to talk about the confidential informant, don't you? In the interest
29 of time, can we skip this testimony?

30   MS. CONNELL: Of course, Your Honor. Officer, you were assigned to
31 investigate this case, weren't you?

32   A.   Yes, I was.

33   Q.   Between the time of the robbery and November 20, YR–02, did
34 you get any information about who committed these crimes?

35   A.   I interviewed some folks on the street who sometimes hear
36 rumors and who occasionally give me some information. Word on the
37 street ...

38   MR. RUSSELL: I have to object, Your Honor. This is irrelevant to any
39 possible legal issue in this case.

40   THE COURT: Sustained. Ms. Connell, I am not sure where you are
41 going with this.

42   MS. CONNELL: Okay, officer, what did you learn on November 20,
43 YR-02 relevant to this case?

1 A. I got a call from a CI.

2 Q. A CI?

3 A. A confidential informant.

4 Q. Was this someone whom you knew?

5 A. No. During the months when I was working the case, I put the
6 word out on the street that I was looking for information. This person
7 seemed to know that.

8 Q. Did you ask the person for his or her identity?

9 A. I did. And she sounded too scared to give me her name.

10 MR. RUSSELL: Objection. The officer could not see the witness; he
11 has no personal knowledge if she was scared.

12 THE COURT: Let's hear his answer.

13 MS. CONNELL: Officer, how could you tell that she was scared?

14 A. She told me so.

15 Q. Did she indicate why?

16 A. No. I asked. But she said she would not tell me.

17 Q. So what did she tell you?

18 A. She said that she knew I was looking for the perps who did the
19 museum job. She gave me a detailed tip of the plan, how they waited until
20 near closing time in the summer when the museum would be empty. They
21 knew that the museum cut its security force and that usually just a
22 couple of old folks were working as docents. She told me the names of the
23 paintings taken and why they were taken. And she told me that Basso
24 was the guy who planned it and was one of the guys who did the job.

25 Q. Did she tell you anything else about the planned crime?

26 A. She said that she thought that the backup plan was to break in
27 after the place closed for the night, in case too many security guards were
28 on hand. She said Basso knew how to disarm the security.

29 Q. And what did you do with that information?

30 A. I told Officer Fish. He was in charge of the investigation.

31 Q. You also tried to follow up by interviewing Tony Basso, didn't
32 you?

33 A. I did.

34 Q. We have heard about the shootout that took place. Have you
35 been charged with any crime arising out the shootout?

36 A. No. I was not even placed on leave.

37 Q. You tried to interview Basso, am I correct?

38 A. Yes, we did.

39 Q. Did you say anything to him about what you wanted to talk
40 about before the shootout?

41 A. Yes, we let him know that we wanted to talk about the museum
42 heist. That is when he pulled a pistol and started shooting.

1   Q. Let me jump to March 27, YR–01. You were on the scene of the
2   search of the defendant's apartment, weren't you?

3   A. I was.

4   Q. Would you tell the court what you did on that occasion?

5   A. Yes. I entered along with Officer Fish. The defendant let us in
6   without a problem. Officer Capone cuffed the defendant. He was playing
7   it nice and just sat there while we made a quick sweep to be sure that this
8   was a secure facility. And then, while Al stayed with the defendant, Fish
9   and I searched the apartment.

10   Q. What, if anything, did you find?

11   A. I found a set of burglary tools.

12   Q. What specifically did you find?

13   A. A set of six flathead screwdrivers in a small case and a six piece
14 BROCKAGE brand set of locksmith tools.

15   Q. Where did you find them?

16   A. I found them in the back bedroom.

17   Q. Specifically, where did you find them?

18   A. Under a dresser.

19   Q. Thank you, Officer. I have nothing further.

20   CROSS EXAMINATION

21   MR. RUSSELL: Well, officer, you told us today a lot of information
22 about the informant. Never mind. I just want to ask you about the infor-
23 mation that the CI gave you. She did not tell you anything about the
24 defendant, did she? I mean she only mentioned Basso as the perp, cor-
25 rect?

26   A. No. She said the other guy was another Basso goon.

27   Q. Was that her description of the other guy?

28   A. Yeah. Big, mean and hairy.

29   Q. Okay. And then when you were executing the warrant, you found
30 the tools in the bedroom. Why did you take the screwdrivers?

31   A. They are a common burglar tool.

32   Q. But this was not a burglary, was it?

33   A. No. But my CI told me that the perps had a backup plan.

34   Q. Was anything special about these screwdrivers that showed they
35 might have special use in this crime?

36   A. We know now that the docent's blood is on one of the screwdriv-
37 ers.

38   MR. RUSSELL: Judge, I guess I asked the question, but the officer's
39 answer is not responsive.

40   THE COURT: Do you dispute the blood evidence? Is that going to
41 come into evidence today?

1   MR. RUSSELL: No; but of course that is why Ms. Connell wants the
2 screwdrivers admitted at trial.

3   THE COURT: So, where is the harm in the officer's answer?

4   MR. RUSSELL: I see. I will continue. Officer, I don't have a picture
5 of the defendant's apartment with me. But would you tell me about the
6 dresser where you found the tools and screwdrivers; I mean how big a
7 dresser.

8   A. Normal size.

9   Q. Well, is it a tall one? And how wide?

10   A. (Indicating) About this tall and yo wide.

11   MR. RUSSELL: For the record, Your Honor, he is indicating about
12 five feet tall, isn't he? And about three feet wide?

13   THE COURT: That looks about right.

14   MR. RUSSELL: And how high off the ground is the dresser; from
15 what I can tell, this is not a really big dresser, high off the ground?

16   A. No. About this high. (Indicating).

17   Q. Again, for the record, he is indicating that the dresser was about
18 a foot off the ground.

19   THE COURT: Yes, that is about right.

20   MR. RUSSELL: So, as you walked into the room, if a six foot tall
21 cardboard tube was under the dresser, you would have seen it immedi-
22 ately, wouldn't you?

23   A. Maybe.

24   Q. Was there some visual obstruction so that you could not have
25 seen the tube?

26   A. No, I guess not.

27   MR. RUSSELL: Thank you, Officer. I have nothing further.

28   THE COURT: Ms. Connell, I hope that we are almost done. If not, I
29 don't think that we will have time to hear argument this afternoon. I
30 don't want to have to put this off any longer.

31   MS. CONNELL: Nothing further, Your Honor.

32   THE COURT: Officer, you may step down. Well, here is how we will
33 proceed. Ms. Connell, you need to address the first issue. I want you to
34 address the search question. Then if I rule against you on that question,
35 Mr. Russell has to convince me that the warrant fails. Then we will get to
36 the third problem, whether the search exceeded the scope of the warrant.
37 My question for both of you is whether you can argue today. This case has
38 been on my calendar for some time. Do you need more time to prepare?

39   MS. CONNELL: I apologize, but I would like to do some additional
40 research, and if Your Honor would permit, I would like to submit a memo-
41 randum of points and authorities as well.

42   THE COURT: What about you, Mr. Russell? Do you want to submit
43 more paper in this case?

1   MR. RUSSELL: Your Honor, I agree with Ms. Connell. Briefing the
2   main points would be helpful. We can't do the argument justice in the
3   time that we have before 5:00 today.

4   THE COURT: We can work past 5:00. Oh well, okay. Check with my
5   clerk for a briefing schedule and hearing date.

CHAPTER THREE

VEHICLE SEARCHES

I. INTRODUCTION

The simulation exercise in this chapter gives you an opportunity to explore the rules governing automobile searches. The chapter includes a brief overview of the law governing automobile searches, a background of the events leading to the search of the defendant's vehicle, the defendant's motion to suppress evidence found by the police, the defendant's memorandum of points and authorities, descriptions of the roles of two police officers and a tow truck driver, police regulations governing inventory searches, and two police forms (an arrest report and inventory form).

II. AN OVERVIEW OF THE LAW

Police search vehicles in a number of settings. In some instances, the police have probable cause to search for evidence in the vehicle. In those cases, the question may be whether the police need a search warrant. The answer has varied over time, as is the case with many Fourth Amendment questions. In recent years, the Court has come close to adopting a bright line rule: searches of vehicles do not require warrants. Unless another rule applies, the police need probable cause to search the vehicle or in a particular area in the vehicle. *See, e.g., California v. Acevedo,* 500 U.S. 565 (1991); *California v. Carney,* 471 U.S. 386 (1985). Other rules governing searches still apply: for example, the police may search only in areas where the object sought may be found.

Even apart from probable cause to believe that evidence may be in a vehicle, the police may justify a search of the vehicle if the search is made incident to a lawful arrest. The Court has struggled with the scope of such searches generally and specifically as such searches relate to vehicles. For example, in 1981, the Court seemingly adopted a bright line rule. In *New York v. Belton*, 453 U.S. 454 (1981), the Court held the scope of a search incident to a lawful arrest of an occupant (or recent occupant) of a vehicle included the interior of the passenger compartment of the vehicle. The rule proved neither particularly bright nor justified: in many cases, the searches could not be justified by the need to protect the arresting officer or by the need to protect evidence of the crime of arrest. *Thornton v. United States,* 541 U.S. 615 (2004) (Scalia, J. concurring). In 2009, the Court "reinterpreted" *Belton* and now requires, in effect, that the police face a continuing threat or a need to preserve evidence before an officer can conduct the search of the vehicle based on the search-incident-to-lawful arrest theory. *Arizona v. Gant,* 556 U.S. 332 (2009).

Vehicles often come under police control not as a result of a criminal investigation, but, for example, when the vehicle must be towed from a public street. Justified by the need to protect the owner of the vehicle and the police, inventory searches are judged by standards of reasonableness. In cases like *Colorado v. Bertine,* 479 U.S. 367 (1987) and *South Dakota v. Opperman,* 428 U.S. 364 (1976), the Court set out rules governing such inventory searches and emphasized the need for standardized procedures. *See also Florida v. Wells,* 495 U.S. 1 (1990).

The scope of a search of a vehicle depends on the justification upon which the state relies. The following problem should help you recognize that point.

III. BACKGROUND

A police officer in the state of Pacific arrested Defendant Steven Wolf for driving while under the influence of alcohol. After taking Wolf into custody and before the arrival of a truck to tow Wolf's van to an impoundment lot, another officer went through the contents of the van. The officer found a backpack behind the front seat of the van. After opening the closed pack, the officer found a metal canister. Opening the canister, the officer discovered that it contained cocaine, methaqualone tablets, cocaine paraphernalia, and $1000 in cash. In an outside zippered pouch of the backpack, he also found $210 in cash in a sealed envelope. After completing the inventory of the van, the officer had the van towed to an impound lot and brought the backpack, money, and contraband to the police station.

Wolf has been indicted for driving while under the influence of alcohol,[1] unlawful possession of cocaine with intent to distribute,[2] and unlawful possession of methaqualone.[3]

The state may rely on McGeorge City police regulations governing inventories, which appear below, United States Supreme Court cases allowing a search of a vehicle incident to a lawful arrest, or United States Supreme Court cases allowing a warrantless search of a vehicle based on probable cause to search. The defendant's counsel filed a motion to suppress the evidence seized from the vehicle. Because the police did not procure a warrant,

---

1. According to § 23152(a) of the Pacific Motor Vehicle Code, driving under the influence of alcohol is defined as follows: "It is unlawful for any person who is under the influence of any alcoholic beverage or drug to drive a vehicle." Subsection (b) provides that "it is unlawful for any person who has 0.08 percent or more, by weight, of alcohol in his or her blood to drive a vehicle."

2. According to § 111351 of the Pacific Health & Safety Code, "every person who possesses any Schedule II controlled substance with intent to distribute shall be punished by imprisonment in the state prison for three, six or nine years." Cocaine is a Schedule II drug. The state proves the intent to distribute by showing that the defendant possesses an amount in excess of what one would possess for personal use.

3. According to § 111350 of the Pacific Health & Safety Code, "every person who possesses any Schedule II controlled substance shall be punished by imprisonment in the county jail for not more than one year or in state prison."

the state must establish the warrantless search was lawful and will put on evidence to prove the legality of the search. The state will present testimony of two police officers and the tow truck driver.

IV. THE MOTION TO SUPPRESS AND MEMORANDUM IN SUPPORT OF THE MOTION

In the
SUPERIOR COURT
FOR THE COUNTY OF McGEORGE

State of Pacific
Plaintiff

Criminal Action No. 00–386 JDS

vs.

Judge: *Michael Vitiello*

Steven Wolf
Defendant

I.   Defendant's Motion to Suppress

Defendant, being a person aggrieved by an unlawful arrest, search and seizure, moves to suppress for use as evidence all items obtained by said arrest, search and seizure and all other evidence obtained as a result thereof on the following grounds:

1.   On January 6, YR–00, the Defendant was arrested and his van was searched by officers of the McGeorge City Police Department.

2.   The Defendant's warrantless arrest was made without probable cause.

3.   The search was conducted without a search warrant and without probable cause to search for evidence or contraband.

4.   The police have alleged that the search was justified by the inventory search exception to the legal requirements for a search warrant, also as a search incident to lawful arrest, and based on probable to cause to believe that evidence was in said backpack.

5.   During the search the police seized and searched a closed backpack and other closed containers found therein. The contents of the closed containers found in the Defendant's van are the controlled substances alleged in the charges herein.

6.   The search of Defendant's van was not pursuant to a valid inventory search, search incident to lawful arrest or based on probable cause to search.

7. For the above reasons and otherwise, the search and seizure was in violation of the Fourth and Fourteenth Amendments of the United States Constitution.

Dated: February 6, YR–00

Respectfully submitted,

Erie Pearson

Erie Pearson
Attorney-at-Law
123 Blackacre Rd.
Telephone: (797) 555–1256
Attorney for Defendant

In the
SUPERIOR COURT
FOR THE COUNTY OF McGEORGE

State of Pacific
Plaintiff

Criminal Action No. 00–386 JDS

vs.

Judge: _Michael Vitiello_

Steven Wolf
Defendant

Memorandum of Points and Authorities on Behalf of Defendant Steven Wolf

I. Introduction

STEVEN WOLF was indicted for possession of cocaine with intent to distribute, possession of methaqualone with intent to distribute, and driving under the influence of alcohol.

II. Facts

On January 6, YR–00, a McGeorge City Police Officer Baker stopped and arrested defendant Steven Wolf for driving under the influence of alcohol. After Mr. Wolf failed a field sobriety test, Officer Baker called for a backup unit. After Mr. Wolf was placed in a police vehicle and taken from the scene, Officer Abel conducted a search of Mr. Wolf's vehicle. He found a half empty beer can. He also found a backpack in Mr. Wolf's vehicle and searched the backpack where he found several hundred dollars, a closed tin labeled Sonoma Mulling Spices, and a closed pouch. Officer Abel opened both the tin and the pouch where he found cocaine, methaqualone, and drug paraphernalia.

Thereafter, Mr. Wolf was indicted for possession of cocaine with intent to distribute, possession of methaqualone with intent to distribute, and driving under the influence of alcohol.

III. Argument

A search conducted without a warrant is per se unreasonable subject to only a few established and well-delineated exceptions. If an exception applies, the burden is on the party seeking the exemption to show the need for it. A warrant is not needed for the search of a vehicle that is parked on a public street, but the police must nonetheless have probable cause to search the vehicle and demonstrate that evidence for which they have probable cause may be located in the place where they search. While the police in this case did not need a warrant, they lacked probable cause to search the vehicle and, more specifically, in the backpack where the evidence was found.

Alternatively, the police may search a vehicle subsequent to a lawful arrest. But the scope of that search has been severely limited by _Arizona v. Gant_, 556 U.S. 332 (2009). The search of defendant's vehicle cannot be justified as a lawful search incident to his arrest.

Finally, a search of a vehicle may be justified as part of a proper inventory. Police must have in place valid procedures to limit officers' discretion, and the officers must follow those procedures. The McGeorge City Police Regulations are so overly broad as to provide no guidance at all. Further, Officer Abel did not comply with those procedures in conducting the purported inventory search in this case.

IV. Conclusion

For the foregoing reasons, defendant requests the court to suppress all of the evidence obtained as a result of the search of defendant's vehicle.

Respectfully submitted,

Erie Pearson

Erie Pearson

Attorney-at-Law
123 Blackacre Road
McGeorge, Pacific 95817
Telephone (797) 555–1256
Attorney for Defendant Steven Wolf

V. WITNESS ROLES

A. John Abel, First Officer:

This is a summary of the facts for the first officer:

You are a member of the McGeorge City Police Department and have been for three years. On January 6, YR–00, in the early morning hours, you received a call from the police dispatcher that Officer Jane Baker requested backup because she was about to arrest a suspect for drunk driving and needed someone to deal with the suspect's vehicle (a van). Once you arrived at the scene, Baker told you the following: she saw Wolf driving at a high rate of speed. She followed him briefly and determined that he exceeded the speed limit by 10 MPH and his vehicle was weaving. Baker pulled him over at the corner of Broadway and College avenues. The roadway is only two lanes without parking on the right side of Broadway where she stopped Wolf. Wolf failed a field sobriety test. He was unable to complete basic tasks like standing on one leg and counting backwards from 25 to 1. He also smelled of alcohol.

Before Baker placed Wolf in handcuffs, she asked you to search Wolf's van. You began to search when you realized that Wolf had a dog in the van. Instead of finishing the search, you called for an animal control unit to deal with the dog. At that point, Baker placed Wolf in her vehicle and took him to the station to be charged with driving under the influence of alcohol.

The animal control unit arrived about 15 minutes later and removed the dog from the van. You then began the search of the van. You decided to have the vehicle impounded because it was on a public roadway without legal on-street parking. Prior to having the vehicle towed, you decided to fill out an inventory form while you searched the vehicle. You decided to do the inventory because of the need to protect yourself and the tow truck company from claims by the owner that something was missing, and to protect yourself, the tow truck company and the public from weapons or explosives that might be in the vehicle.

You filled out the inventory form but omitted a few items, like an envelope labeled rent, which contained several hundred dollars. But you did list the following items: one half empty can of beer, a backpack and additional items, found in the backpack, including a tin labeled Sonoma Mulling Spices and a pouch. You opened both of those items. In the tin, you found a substance you determined was cocaine and another substance found to be methaqualone. In the pouch, you found items related to the use of illegal drugs, including a pipe (a little glass tube) for smoking cocaine, a small mirror and a razor blade for processing cocaine.

In conducting the inventory, you were trying to comply with the police regulations governing inventories. See the attached regulations. But you were also fairly sure that you were justified to search the vehicle even if it was not based on the inventory procedure. Also, you have conducted a number of vehicle searches and found perhaps as many as 50 backpacks during those searches. Typically, they contain valuable personal items and occasionally dangerous items, like knives and handguns.

B. Jane Baker, Second Officer

This is a summary of the facts for the second officer:

You are a member of the McGeorge City Police Department and have been for five years. On January 6, YR–00, in the early morning hours, you arrested Steven Wolf. You are able to identify him in court as the defendant. You were in your patrol car when you saw Wolf drive by at a high rate of speed. Wolf was driving a YR–07 Chrysler mini-van. You followed his van briefly, determined he was exceeding the speed limit by 10 MPH and his vehicle was weaving. You pulled him over at the corner of Broadway and College avenues. The roadway is only two lanes without parking on the right side of Broadway where you stopped Wolf. Before you approached Wolf, you called for backup because you concluded that you would make a custodial arrest of the driver. You asked Wolf for his license and registration and noticed the odor of alcohol. You asked him to get out of his vehicle and to do a field sobriety test. He was unable to complete basic tasks like standing on one leg and counting backwards from 25 to 1. At that point, back-up (Officer Abel) arrived at the scene. You told Abel the facts above.

Before you placed Wolf in handcuffs, you asked Abel to search Wolf's van. At that point, you placed Wolf in your vehicle and took him to the station to be charged with driving under the influence of alcohol.

C. Rusty Crow, Tow Truck Driver

This is a summary of the facts for the tow truck driver:

You are employed by Western Pacific Chevrolet. WPC has a contract with the city of McGeorge whereby WPC's tow truck drivers remove impounded vehicles from public streets upon the request of the police. Further, WPC secures the vehicles in its lot until the owner can provide evidence that the court has ordered its release. WPC has a security fence surrounding the vehicle lot and a contract with a private security firm to check the lot periodically. A six-foot chain link fence surrounds the lot. Hiring the security firm was required by the contract with the city. On January 6, YR–00, you received a call that the McGeorge police had arrested a suspect and needed a tow truck operator to impound the vehicle. You responded to the call and towed a YR–07 Chrysler mini-van to WPC's lot.

VI. POLICE REGULATIONS

McGEORGE CITY POLICE DEPARTMENT
OFFICE OF THE CHIEF OF POLICE GENERAL PROCEDURE
DATE ISSUED: 07/19/YR–1
DATE EFFECTIVE: 09/07/YR–1
EXPIRATION: Indefinite
SUBJECT OF PROCEDURE: MOTOR VEHICLE IMPOUNDS
TO: ALL DEPARTMENT PERSONNEL

Purpose:

To ensure the appropriate care and security of motor vehicles taken into custody by the Department.

I.   Procedures

A.   Upon placing a motor vehicle in Police custody, Officers shall take the following steps in securing the vehicle and its contents:

1.   If the vehicle is the fruit of a crime, the Officer shall conduct a detailed vehicle inspection and inventory and record it upon the VEHICLE IMPOUND FORM.

2.   Personal items of value should be removed from the vehicle and subsequently placed into Property for safekeeping.

3.   The Officer shall request a Tow Truck, and upon its arrival have the Tow Truck operator sign the IMPOUND FORM, keeping one copy in his possession, before the Officer releases the vehicle for impoundment in the McGeorge City impoundment facility.

B.   The above procedure shall be followed when a vehicle involved in a traffic accident is to be held for evidentiary purposes.

C.   In all other cases, the Officer may follow these procedures, may have the vehicle towed to the impoundment lot before conducting the inventory or may follow those stated in II, below.

II.   Park and Lock Procedures:

Upon placing the operator of a motor vehicle in custody, Officers may take the following steps in securing the arrestee's vehicle and property IF THE FOLLOWING CONDITIONS ARE PRESENT:

1.   The vehicle and/or its contents ARE NOT themselves the fruit of a crime.

2.   The vehicle has not been involved in a traffic accident requiring its impoundment as evidence.

If the above conditions exist, the Officer may take the following steps to secure the vehicle:

1. Conduct a detailed vehicle inspection and inventory and record it upon a VEHICLE IMPOUND FORM. When possible, have a second Officer witness this inventory.

2. Closed containers that give no indication of containing either valuables or a weapon may not be opened and the contents searched. (i.e., inventoried)

3. Personal items of value will be removed from the vehicle and subsequently placed into PROPERTY for safekeeping.

4. The Officer shall drive the vehicle off the roadway and legally park the vehicle in the nearest PUBLIC parking area. The date, time, and location where the vehicle is parked shall be indicated on the IMPOUND FORM.

5. The Officer shall remove the ignition keys and lock all doors of the vehicle.

6. During the booking process, the arrestee shall be given a continuation form for his signature that indicates the location of his vehicle. One copy of the continuation form is to be retained in the case file.

7. The arrestee shall be advised of the procedures required in obtaining personal property removed from the vehicle and placed into Property for safekeeping, i.e., TV's, valuables, etc.

8. The ignition key to the vehicle should remain with the items that are transported with the arrestee should this individual be incarcerated.

NOTE: Routine Motor Vehicle Impoundment Procedures should be used if no public parking areas exist in the immediate vicinity of the arrest, there is reasonable risk of damage or vandalism to the vehicle, or the arrested individual requests that the vehicle be impounded in the City's storage facility.

C. If the aforementioned conditions exist the Officer may, at his discretion, release the vehicle to a present individual designated by the arrestee after ownership is shown to be held by this individual, and the person so indicated shows proof of holding a valid motor vehicle operator's license.

McGEORGE COUNTY SHERIFFS DEPARTMENT

DATE: PRINTED	**Jan. 6, YR-00**		**ARREST REPORT**	PAGE	**1**
				TIME	**14:30**

ARREST:

NAME:	**Steven Wolf**			DOB:	**5-6-YR-26**
CASE:	**00814**	AGENCY:	**McGeorge PD**	SUBJECT:	
DATE OF ARREST:	**1-6-YR-00**	TIME OF ARREST:	**0020**	PID:	

CHG :01

OFF:	**Possession of schedule 2 controlled substances**			STATUTE:	**Pacific Penal Code 13-879**
CATEGORY:	**Felony**	CLASS:	**3**	SUMMONS:	
DATE OF OFFENSE:	**1-6-YR-00**	TIME OF OFFENSE:	**0020**	DOC:	
BOND TYPE:		BOND AMOUNT:		BOND OK?	
CONDITIONS OF BOND:					
COMMENTS:					
NEXT APPEARANCE: DATE:		TIME:		PURPOSE:	
JURISDICTION TYPE:		JURISDICTION NAME:		DIV:	

CHG :02

OFF:	**DUI**			STATUTE:	**PPC-13-1202**
CATEGORY:	**Misdemeanor**	CLASS:	**2**	SUMMONS:	
DATE OF OFFENSE:		TIME OF OFFENSE:		DOC:	
BOND TYPE:		BOND AMOUNT:		BOND OK?	
CONDITIONS OF BOND:					
COMMENTS:					
NEXT APPEARANCE: DATE:		TIME:		PURPOSE:	
JURISDICTION TYPE:		JURISDICTION NAME:		DIV:	

ARRESTEE:

ADULT PID:						RECORD TYPE:	**Arrest**			
NAME:	**Steven Wolf**							DOB:	**5-6-YR-26**	
ALIAS	**Skunk**							AGE AT OFF:	**25**	
RAC: **W**	SEX: **M**	HGT: **68'**	WGT: **160**	HAI	brown	EYE: brown	MARITAL:	single	SSN:	123-45-6789
WORK:	**unemployed**									
POB:			DRIVER LIC:	**B9823890**			ST:	**Pacific**	EXP:	**YR+2**
SCARS ETC:										
CLOTHING DESCRIPTION:	**Blue jeans, flannel shirt, leather jacket**									
FINGERPRINT CLASS:										
FBI:								AGENCY:	**09016**	

HOME ADD:	**546 Wayside Drive** **McGeorge City**	APT #:	PHONE:	
LOC ARRST:		APT #:	PHONE:	
LOC OFFNS:		APT #:	PHONE:	

NARRATIVE:

At approximately 0020 HRS., on 1-6-YR-00, Officer Jane Baker observed the Def.'s vehicle, a 2004 Chrysler van, traveling erratically at a high rate of speed. OJB pulled over suspect vehicle at corner of Broadway and College Avenues. OJB asked for Def.'s license and registration; in doing so, she smelled odor of alcohol. OJB asked Def. to exit vehicle to take field sobriety. He failed test.

Back up officer John Abel, at request of OJB, searched vehicle. Because Abel discovered a canine in vehicle, he called for animal control vehicle. After animal control removed canine, Abel conducted a search and filled inventory form. Among other items, Abel found a back pack containing tin can of mulling spices and a pouch. Both contained illegal narcotics and drug paraphernalia.

NARRATIVE CONTINUED

VEHICLE:

STATUS:	**Impound**		IMPOUND LOCATION:	**Western Pacific Chevrolet**		
YEAR:	**2004**	MCD:		STY: **van**		
VIN:	**1468TV043**		COLORS **tan**			
LIC NUM:	**Bong21**	LIC ST: **Pacific**		LIC TYP **PC**	LIC EXP	**YR+2**

MISC: **Arrest Officer: Jane Baker Badge 998   Agency McGeroge PD**

VEHICLE IMPOUND REPORT

| | | Impound Number | YR-00 16 |

Reporting Agency

X☐ McGeorge City Police Department
☐ McGeorge County Sheriff's Department

☐ Other _____

CASE NUMBER | |

	Date of Impound	Time	Location Impound From			
1	1-6-YR-00	0020	Broadway and College Avenues			

| 2 | TYPE | ☐ STOLEN | X☐ ARREST | ☐ HIT/RUN | ☐ 72 HOUR | ☐ ABANDONED | ☐ OTHER |

VEHICLE DESCRIPTION

	Make	Model	Body	Year	Vin
3	Chrysler	Caravan	Van	YR-07	101SM9756

	Front License Plate	State	Year	Rear License Plate	State	Year
4	None			BONG21	Pacific	YR-07

	Color(s) (Top to Bottom)	Speedometer Reading
5	Green	

| 6 | x NCIC CHECK | X CCIC CHECK | TO BE RELEASED x☐ YES ☐ NO | HOLD FOR: |

VEHICLE CONDITION (Indicate damage)	PROPERTY INVENTORIED (items of value)		
Dents front left panel	DESCRIPTION	SERIAL	CODE
	Jumper cables		
	backpack		
	pouch		
	cocaine		
	pills		
	pipe		

NARRATIVE, DESCRIPTION OF CIRCUMSTANCES:

	Officer making impound		No	Date	Time
7	John Abel		163	1-6-YR-00	003
8	Vehicle Received by Name of Towing Service Western Pacific	Name of Driver Rusty Crow		Date 1-6-YR-00	Time 003
9	Vehicle Released from impound to:	Address		Date	Time

CHAPTER FOUR

PROBABLE CAUSE, SEARCH INCIDENT TO LAWFUL ARREST AND BEYOND

I. INTRODUCTION

The simulation exercise in this chapter gives you an opportunity to explore the rules governing four different doctrines. The first issue is whether the police have probable cause to arrest the defendant. The second issue deals with the scope of the search incident to lawful arrest doctrine. Specifically, it introduces you to a conflict among lower courts when the object of the police search is a cell phone. The third issue relates to the fruit of the poisonous tree. That is, to what extent does an initial, illegal arrest make a subsequent statement inadmissible? The fourth issue focuses on *Miranda* rights and whether the police violated those rights, even on the assumption that the earlier conduct did not violate the Fourth Amendment.

This chapter consists a brief overview of the law governing the issues described above, a discussion of the role of counsel in this exercise, the defendant's motion to suppress evidence, a short memorandum in support of that motion, and a transcript of a hearing on the defendant's motion to suppress evidence.

II. OVERVIEW OF THE LAW

A. Probable Cause

In the simulation, the police have received an anonymous tip suggesting that the defendant has engaged in a drug deal. Under the Warren Court's precedent, if the police sought to rely on an anonymous tip, the police had to demonstrate the reliability of the informant and the basis of the informant's knowledge. *Spinelli v. United States,* 393 U.S. 410 (1969). Failing that, the police had to corroborate the tip to shore up the inadequate prong of the test. According to the Court in *Illinois v. Gates,* 462 U.S. 213 (1983), *Spinelli's* test was unnecessarily begrudging and produced confusion among lower courts. In *Gates*, the Court replaced the test for determining probable cause with a totality of the circumstances test. As stated there, the trial court must conduct a "balanced assessment of the relative weights of all the various indicia of reliability (and unreliability) attending an informant's tip." The concept of probable cause is "fluid," based on "the factual and practical considerations of everyday life on which reasonable and prudent men, not legal technicians, act." The concept is not reducible to a set of legal rules.

The Court has indicated that the rules governing probable cause apply with equal force whether the issue is probable cause to arrest or to search. Of course, probable cause to arrest focuses on whether the police have sufficient cause to believe that the defendant has committed a crime, while probable cause to search goes to whether the police have sufficient cause to believe that evidence of a crime will be found where the police seek to search.

B. Search Incident to Lawful Arrest

The Court's rules governing the scope of a lawful search incident to a lawful arrest are deceptively straightforward. The Warren Court narrowed earlier precedent in *Chimel v. California,* 395 U.S. 752 (1969). While *Chimel* dealt with the scope of a search incident to a lawful arrest made in the defendant's home—not the situation in the simulation—the Court's approach was typical of the Warren Court. *Chimel* started with the proposition that the Fourth Amendment required that the police have probable cause and a warrant unless the police conduct came within a narrow exception to that rule. To keep those exceptions narrow, the Court looked to the underlying justification for creating an exception to its general rule. A search incident to lawful arrest was justified by the need to protect officers and to prevent suspects from destroying evidence. Hence, in *Chimel*, the police could not roam about the house after the suspect was under arrest.

By the early 1970's—after four new appointments to the Court—the Court's approach to the Fourth Amendment generally, and the search incident doctrine specifically, began to change. Thus, in *United States v. Robinson,* 414 U.S. 218 (1973), the Court held that the search incident to lawful arrest of a suspect included the suspect's person and, in that case, a crumpled cigarette package (that contained capsules of heroin). What made the case difficult, in part, was the fact that the offense (driving on a suspended license) did not involve evidence that might be destroyed. In addition, the officer did not fear for his safety and could easily have limited the search by conducting a patdown for a weapon. The Court held the search was lawful. It so held, in part, because of the need to create clear rules to govern police conduct.

Not long thereafter, the Court held a search was justified as a search incident to lawful arrest even when the search did not take place until several hours after the initial arrest. In *United States v. Edwards,* 415 U.S. 800 (1974), the defendant was in police custody. The police suspected him of breaking and entering and realized that his clothing might contain evidence of the illegal entry. The search did not take place until ten hours after his initial arrest. The Court upheld the warrantless search and observed that "searches that could be made on the spot at the time of arrest may legally be conducted later when the accused arrives at the place of detention." The analytical framework in cases like *Robinson* and *Edwards* focuses on the reasonableness of the police conduct, not on narrowly tailoring the exception to the underlying justifications for the exception to the warrant requirement.

There are limits to *Edwards'* rule. In *United States v. Chadwick,* 433 U.S. 1 (1977), F.B.I. agents seized the defendant's 200–pound footlocker during a lawful arrest. By the time the case got to the Supreme Court, the government took a position found to be extreme, that the warrant requirement applied only to searches of homes. But the Court discussed the search incident to arrest rationale nonetheless. It noted that the search did not take place contemporaneously with the arrest and observed that once the police reduced the property "not immediately associated with the person of the arrestee to their exclusive control, and there is no longer any danger that the arrestee might gain access to the property to seize a weapon or destroy evidence, a search of that property is no longer an incident of the arrest." Presumably, the latter language distinguishes a case like *Robinson* or *Edwards* from a case like *Chadwick*. But it suggests some of the confusion that the Court's case law has caused among lower courts.

One other set of cases suggests the analytical problems associated with the Court's search incident to lawful arrest case law. In 1981, the Court seemingly adopted a bright line rule governing the doctrine when the search involved an automobile. In *New York v. Belton*, 453 U.S. 454 (1981), the Court held that the scope of a search incident to a lawful arrest of an occupant (or recent occupant) of a vehicle included the interior of the passenger compartment of the vehicle. The rule proved neither particularly bright nor justified: in many cases, the searches could not be justified by the need to protect the arresting officer. Nor could they be justified by the need to protect evidence of the crime of arrest. *Thornton v. United States,* 541 U.S. 615 (2004) (Scalia, J. concurring). In 2009, the Court "reinterpreted" *Belton* and now requires, in effect, that the police face a continuing threat or a need to preserve evidence before an officer can conduct the search of vehicle based on the search incident to lawful arrest theory. *Arizona v. Gant,* 556 U.S. 332 (2009).

Justice Stevens' majority in *Gant* harkens back to the Warren Court formulation of the Fourth Amendment: the Fourth Amendment requires that the police have probable cause and a search warrant unless the police conduct comes within a narrow exception to the general rule. Further, the opinion emphasized that, on the facts before the Court, (with the suspect handcuffed in a police car and under arrest for a crime that did not involve physical evidence), the underlying justifications for the search incident to lawful arrest rule were not advanced by allowing the search. Whether the Court intends to apply that kind of reasoning in areas outside the automobile context has yet to be determined.

C. Rights under *Miranda v. Arizona*

Miranda v. Arizona, 384 U.S. 436 (1966), held that the police must give a suspect a set of warnings when the police engage in custodial interrogation. Those warnings include a warning that the suspect has a right to remain silent, that anything the suspect says can be used against him, that he has a right to have counsel present during an interrogation, and that he has a right to have counsel appointed if the suspect cannot afford counsel. Further, the police must secure a voluntary waiver of those rights before the police may interrogate the suspect.

Controversial for many years, *Miranda* has spawned a substantial body of case law interpreting almost every aspect of the original holding. For example, the Court has created an exception not requiring warnings when the police ask the suspect booking questions. *Pennsylvania v. Muniz,* 496 U.S. 582 (1990). The Court has held that "interrogation" includes not only express questioning but also its "functional equivalent." *Rhode Island v. Innis,* 446 U.S. 291 (1980). While a waiver of *Miranda* rights must be voluntary, the Court applies a case-by-case analysis and has provided no clear guidance on how to assess such a claim. Further, the *Miranda* Court did not require an express waiver but also stated that a waiver should not be inferred from a silent record. Recently, the Court seems to have found a *Miranda* waiver on just such a silent record in *Berghuis v. Thompkins,* 560 U.S. ___ (2010).

D. Fruits of the Poisonous Tree

As a general rule, the Court applies the Fourth Amendment's exclusionary rule when the police act illegally and discover physical evidence. When the evidence at issue involves a statement made by the defendant, the law becomes more complicated. That is because the defendant's act of free will may purge the taint of the original illegal conduct. *See, e.g., Wong Sun v. United States,* 371 U.S. 471 (1963). In *Brown v. Illinois,* 422 U.S. 590 (1975), the State argued that *Miranda* warnings and the subsequent waiver of those rights broke the causal link between a Fourth Amendment violation and the defendant's subsequent statement. The Court rejected such a bright line rule. Instead, *Miranda* warnings do not alone make the act of confessing "a product of free will to break, for Fourth Amendment purposes, the causal connection between the illegality and the confession." Instead, the Court relies on a totality of the circumstances test. *See, e.g., Kaupp v. Texas,* 58 U.S. 62 (2003) (per curiam).

III.   PEOPLE v. WALTER MARTINEZ

In this simulation, the People have charged the defendant, Walter Martinez, with one count of the sale of a controlled substance (Vicodin), a violation of the Pacific Health & Safety Code § 11351. That provision makes the sale of a controlled substance a felony, punishable by two, three, or four years in prison. The People have charged Martinez with a second count of the sale of a controlled substance (Methaqualone), also a violation of Health & Safety Code § 11351.

What follows is the defendant's motion to suppress evidence, a brief memorandum supporting his motion, and the transcript of the evidentiary hearing in People v. Martinez.

Your professor will assign one or more students to represent the People and a student or students to serve as defense counsel. Because the court has heard the evidence but not yet made findings of fact, you may argue in favor of particular factual findings (obviously favoring your legal position) and, of course, you should argue the application of those facts to the law. Without a live witness, you cannot argue credibility based on demeanor. But you can argue whether the witnesses' testimony is credible in light of internal inconsistencies and logic. One lesson that you should take from this exercise is that facts are not always as clear as they appear when you read appellate decisions. Indeed, you will see some inconsistencies in the testimony of the two witnesses and within the testimony of one of the witnesses.

More important than factual arguments are the relevant legal arguments. Depending on instructions from your professor, you may argue all of the legal issues in this exercise. You may decide that some of the issues are stronger than others and choose, therefore, to emphasize the strongest arguments that allow you to prevail. Assessing the strength of one's legal argument is itself a critical skill lawyers must learn.

As an alternative to assigning students roles as trial counsel, your professor may use this as a writing assignment or as an appellate argument. The Teacher's Manual includes a trial court opinion that your professor may copy and assign to your class. In that case, you may be assigned to write or argue orally whether the trial court opinion should be reversed.

In the
SUPERIOR COURT
FOR THE COUNTY OF McGEORGE

State of Pacific
Plaintiff

Criminal Action No. 00–13460 JDS

vs.

Judge: Jeremy Taylor

Walter Martinez
Defendant

I.   Defendant's Motion to Suppress

Defendant, being a person aggrieved by an unlawful arrest, search and seizure, moves to suppress for use as evidence all items obtained by said arrest, search and seizure and all other evidence obtained as a result thereof on the following grounds:

1.   On March 10, YR–00, the Defendant was arrested by officers of the McGeorge City Police Department.

2.   The Defendant's warrantless arrest was made without probable cause.

3.   The search was conducted without a search warrant and without probable cause to search for evidence or contraband.

4.   The police have alleged that the search was justified as a search incident to lawful arrest.

5.   The Defendant was arrested for the theft of a bicycle. During the search the police seized and searched two cell phones. When the search was conducted, neither phone was in the possession or control of the Defendant.

6.   Not only were the phones not in the Defendant's control when the search was conducted, but the police had no reason to believe they would find evidence of the theft on the phones or that the phones imperiled their safety.

7.   Further, statements made by the Defendant were either the product of his illegal arrest, the illegal search of his cell phones, or the failure of the police to get a proper waiver of his right to remain silent.

8. For the above reasons and otherwise, the search and seizure was in violation of the Fourth and Fourteenth Amendments under the United States Constitution and the Defendant's inculpatory statements were taken in violation of his Fourth, Fifth and Fourteenth Amendment rights under the United States Constitution.

Dated: May 23, YR–00

> Respectfully submitted,
>
> *Carla Bricker*
>
> Carla Bricker
>
> Attorney-at-Law
> 151 Greenacre Rd.
> Telephone: (797) 555–5768
> Attorney for Defendant

In the
SUPERIOR COURT
FOR THE COUNTY OF McGEORGE

State of Pacific
Plaintiff

Criminal Action No. 00–13460 JDS

vs.

Judge: Jeremy Taylor

Walter Martinez
Defendant

Memorandum of Points and Authorities on Behalf of Defendant

I. Introduction

Walter Martinez was indicted for the sale of Vicodin and the sale of Methaqualone in violation of Health & Safety Code § 11351 on March 31, YR–00.

II. Facts

On March 10, YR–00, two undercover McGeorge City Police Officers, Officers Giuseppe and Jones, stopped and arrested defendant Walter Martinez for the theft of a bicycle. After he was under arrest and already in custody in the police stationhouse, Officer Jones searched Mr. Martinez's cell phones and found evidence that the People contend shows that Mr. Martinez was involved in the illegal sale of controlled substances, to wit, Vicodin and Methaqualone. Confronted with this information and without proper *Miranda* warnings, Mr. Martinez admitted his involvement in the sale of drugs.

Thereafter, Mr. Martinez was indicted for the sale of Vicodin and the sale of Methaqualone.

III. Argument

To comply with the Fourth Amendment, an arrest must be based on probable cause to believe that the defendant has committed a criminal offense. Officers Jones and Giuseppe lacked sufficient information to form such a belief, whether they arrested the defendant for the theft of a bicycle or the sale of controlled substances. On that basis alone, this court must suppress the evidence to be used against Mr. Martinez.

Further, even if the arrest was based on probable cause to believe that Mr. Martinez was guilty of theft, the police had secured both of Mr. Martinez's cell phones. Consistent with the United States Supreme Court decision in *Arizona v. Gant,* 556 U.S. 332 (2009), the police search was illegal under the doctrine of search incident to lawful arrest because the search could not possibly be justified based on the need to protect the officers or to protect against the destruction of the evidence.

Because the arrest of Mr. Martinez and/or search of his cell phones was illegal, his statements to the police must be suppressed as the fruit of the poisonous tree. Further, even if not, his statements must be suppressed because the police did not comply with the clear guidelines set forth in *Miranda v. Arizona,* 384 U.S. 436 (1966) and its progeny.

IV.   Conclusion

For the foregoing reasons, Mr. Martinez requests the court to suppress all of the evidence obtained as a result of his arrest and the search of his cell phones.

Respectfully submitted,

Carla Bricker

Carla Bricker

Attorney-at-Law
151 Greenacre Road
McGeorge, Pacific 95817
Telephone (797) 555–5768
Attorney for Defendant Walter Martinez

1
2   Transcript of Hearing on Defendant Walter Martinez's Motion
           to Suppress

3   Monday, June 26, YR–00

4   The matter of People of the State of Pacific v. Walter Martinez, Defen-
5   dant, case number 00–13460, came before the Honorable Jeremy Taylor,
6   Judge of the Superior Court of Pacific, County of McGeorge.

7   THE COURT: Good morning, ladies and gentlemen. Am I correct that
8   our first case is People v. Martinez?

9   Mr. LEACH: Yes, your honor.

10   THE COURT: Would counsel state their names for the record? And
11   speak clearly. Ms. Lester is a new court reporter, and she appreciates
12   folks who speak clearly.

13   Mr. LEACH: Tom Leach for the State of Pacific.

14   Ms. BRICKER: Carla Bricker for Mr. Martinez.

15   THE COURT: Am I correct that there is no warrant, uh, search war-
16   rant in this case?

17   Mr. LEACH: So stipulated.

18   THE COURT: Also, while we are at this point dealing with adminis-
19   trative details, I have read Ms. Bricker's submissions, her motion and
20   authorities. Mr. Leach, did you file papers?

21   Mr. LEACH: The People did not but obviously we reserve the right to
22   argue the motion and to present evidence.

23   THE COURT: Of course. You know that in my court, I prefer that the
24   prosecution respond in writing before the hearing?

25   Mr. LEACH: With due deference, Your Honor, you know what budget
26   cuts have done to our office. I am sorry. If at the end of the hearing, it
27   becomes necessary, I will present written opposition.

28   THE COURT: We will see about that later. So, let's get started. The
29   air conditioning has not been working so well lately, and the county is
30   trying to save some money by turning up the thermostat. I am sure that
31   everyone here would like to get back to their offices sooner rather than
32   later.

33   Mr. LEACH: The People call Officer Marla Giuseppe.

34   THE COURT: Would you swear the witness?

35   THE CLERK: Do you solemnly swear that the testimony you are
36   about to give in this case shall be the truth, the whole truth, and nothing
37   but the truth, so help you God?

38   OFFICER GIUSEPPE: I do.

39   THE CLERK: Please be seated. And would you spell your name for
40   the record?

41   THE WITNESS: M-a-r-l-a G-i-u-s-e-p-p-e.

42   THE COURT: Ready, Mr. Leach?

43   DIRECT EXAMINATION

44   By Mr. LEACH:

1   Q.   Officer Giuseppe, would you tell us your occupation and how long
2   you have held that position?

3   A.   I have been a police officer for the McGeorge City Police Depart-
4   ment for five years.

5   Q.   Your present assignment is what?

6   A.   Narcotics.

7   Q.   Directing your attention to March 10 of this year, did you receive
8   information about Mr. Martinez?

9   A.   I did.

10   Q.   Officer, what was that information?

11   A.   I received a tip from a confidential informant indicating that she
12   had made a purchase of five Vicodin tablets from the defendant.

13   Q.   When you say "confidential informant," I assume that you mean
14   someone who has provided you with reliable information in the past?

15   Ms. BRICKER: Objection, Your Honor. Mr. Leach is leading the wit-
16   ness.

17   THE COURT: Ms. Bricker, this is going to be a long morning if you
18   have objections like that. Let's see what the officer says.

19   Mr. LEACH: Thank you, Your Honor. Officer, do you need the stenog-
20   rapher to read back the question?

21   THE WITNESS: No. The question was whether this was a reliable
22   informant. But the answer is no. I was in the station; nobody picked up
23   the phone and so I did because the duty sergeant was booking a suspect.

24   Q.   Oh. What did, uh, let me begin again. Did the person identify
25   him or herself?

26   A.   No. But she told me that she bought the pills from the defendant.
27   She named him and told me the corner where he regularly hangs out.

28   Q.   Which was?

29   A.   On Olive Drive, the corner with 5th Street.

30   Q.   Is that a high crime ... uh, I see Ms. Bricker ready to jump out of
31   her seat. Can you describe the neighborhood?

32   A.   It is a high crime area.

33   Ms. BRICKER: Objection, Your Honor. That is highly conclusory.
34   What on earth does that mean and is ...

35   THE COURT: Ms. Bricker, I understand your point. I am not sure
36   that it is worth the time to establish that Olive Drive at 5th Street is a
37   high crime area. I doubt that you take a stroll there on your day off. But
38   Mr. Leach, go ahead and establish why your witness considers that a high
39   crime area.

40   Mr. LEACH: Officer, why do your characterize Olive and 5th a high
41   crime area?

42   THE WITNESS: I have personally made hundreds of drug arrests in
43   that area. It is like the TV series, the Wire, you know? We see the corner
44   boys ...

1   Ms. BRICKER: Objection, Your Honor.

2   THE COURT: Technically, you are correct. But the officer already
3 testified that she has made hundreds of drug arrests there. That is
4 enough, move on Mr. Leach.

5   Mr. LEACH: So when you got the tip, you headed ... I am sorry. What
6 did you do when you got the tip?

7   THE WITNESS: I was working undercover. I got an unmarked car
8 and got Officer Sid Jones to join me. We went to Olive and 5th and saw
9 someone fitting the description of the guy who sold the tipster the Vico-
10 din.

11   Q.   What did you observe before arresting the defendant?

12   Ms. BRICKER: Objection. How do we know that this was the defen-
13 dant?

14   THE COURT: Mr. Leach, I know that I said that we should try to get
15 done this morning but not so many shortcuts. Sustained.

16   Mr. LEACH: Can you identify the person whom you saw on the cor-
17 ner?

18   THE WITNESS: Yes.

19   Q.   Who was it?

20   A.   The defendant.

21   Q.   Were you familiar with the defendant?

22   A.   Sure. I arrested him for selling Oxycontin two or three times over
23 the last year.

24   Q.   So you saw the defendant and.... ?

25   A.   On two occasions, someone came up to him, talked briefly and
26 then he pointed down the street towards 4th Street.

27   Q.   And you assumed, no, let me start again. Did his conduct suggest
28 anything to you?

29   THE COURT: I am sure that Ms. Bricker is about to object. So let me
30 jump in. Officer, you said that you are in the narcotics unit. Have you
31 received training in how to identify drug transactions?

32   A.   Yes, sir.

33   THE COURT: And what did you learn?

34   A.   Well, the kid on the corner is not going to carry drugs. Instead,
35 he will point the buyer to a different location where the buyer can get the
36 drugs. That means the corner boy does not carry drugs so when he is
37 arrested he may be able to deny his involvement. And then he can figure
38 out if he knows the buyer or if the buyer looks like a setup for the police.

39   THE COURT: One more question: have you observed this kind of
40 practice in your several years on the force?

41   A.   Yes. That is exactly the pattern that we witness in that area.

42   THE COURT: Back to work Mr. Leach. I don't want you to fall asleep
43 on me.

1   Mr. LEACH: Thank you, Your Honor. Officer, so after you observed
2 the defendant in what you concluded were drug transactions, did you
3 arrest him at that point for narcotics trafficking?

4   A.   No.

5   Q.   Oh. What did you do?

6   A.   We watched him for awhile until he got ready to leave the area.

7   Q.   What did you see him do then that led to his arrest?

8   A.   The defendant got on a fancy electric bike. It was an Optibike, I
9 think a blue stripped Optibike 700.

10   Q.   And so?

11   A.   These monsters sell for about $8 or 9 grand. I radioed the station
12 while Officer Jones drove behind the defendant. We thought that he must
13 have stolen this bike and bingo, the duty sergeant told me that an
14 Optibike store ten blocks away from where we were driving had been
15 burglarized a few nights earlier. He told me that one of the bikes stolen
16 was a 700 series and it was the same color as the one that the defendant
17 was riding.

18   Q.   And at that point, did you arrest the defendant?

19   A.   We did. We pulled up to a red light where the defendant stopped.
20 Jones stopped the car and hopped out and identified himself, showing the
21 defendant his badge.

22   Q.   And then?

23   A.   Officer Jones told him that he was under arrest for stealing the
24 bike. He told the defendant to turn towards the building on the corner, to
25 spread his legs while Jones patted him down.

26   Q.   What, if anything, did Jones find on the defendant?

27   Ms. BRICKER: Your Honor, I have been biding my time. I assume
28 that Officer Jones will testify about what he found. I saw him in the hall-
29 way when we came in this morning. This seems redundant.

30   THE COURT: Mr. Leach, any response?

31   Mr. LEACH: I would be delighted to move on. Oh, if I may recall the
32 officer if I need to, without objection from Ms. Bricker.

33   Ms. BRICKER: That is fine.

34   Mr. LEACH: I tender the witness.

35   CROSS EXAMINATION

36   Ms. BRICKER: Officer, you said that you observed the defendant on
37 the corner of Olive and 5th and that you watched him for awhile, didn't
38 you?

39   THE WITNESS: Yes, I did.

40   Q.   How long did you watch?

41   A.   Maybe a half hour, 40 minutes.

42   Q.   And in that time, you did not see the defendant hand anyone
43 anything, did you?

1 A. No. I explained that. The corner boys ...

2 Q. I heard your explanation. Stick to the question, please.

3 Mr. LEACH: Objection, argumentative.

4 THE COURT: Sustained. But officer, do try to stick to the question.

5 Ms. BRICKER: You testified that a couple of folks came up to the
6 defendant and that he pointed down the street somewhere, didn't you?

7 THE WITNESS: You got that right.

8 Q. You did not testify what is down the street in the direction that
9 he pointed, did you?

10 A. I don't think that I did. Mr. Leach didn't ask me, did he?

11 Q. Your Honor, would you instruct the witness?

12 THE COURT: Officer, answer the question. Please don't get smart-
13 alecky with the defense counsel. You are just going to prolong these pro-
14 ceedings.

15 THE WITNESS: I am sorry.

16 Ms. BRICKER: So, what was down the street, say past 4th Street?

17 A. A lot of stuff.

18 Q. Isn't that where there is a park with several basketball courts?

19 A. I guess so. I don't know that neighborhood all that well.

20 Q. Oh, didn't you testify that you knew that neighborhood well, that
21 you knew that it was a high crime area? That is what you testified to,
22 wasn't it?

23 A. Sure.

24 Q. So, aren't you aware of the park, a place where dozens of kids
25 hang out, you missed that somehow?

26 A. No. I guess I know the park you are describing.

27 Q. And then further along 4th Street, aren't you aware of several
28 restaurants and donut shops? Surely, you know about the donut shops,
29 don't you?

30 Mr. LEACH: Please, Your Honor, would you instruct Ms. Bricker to be
31 less argumentative?

32 THE COURT: Please, Mr. Leach and Ms. Bricker, can we get to the
33 core of the matter? You don't have to be cute with the witness and Mr.
34 Leach, the officer does not need you to take care of her.

35 Ms. BRICKER: Thank you, Your Honor. I assume that I may resume?

36 (The Court nods).

37 Q. So you are familiar with the restaurants and shops?

38 A. Yes.

39 Q. So from what you observed, the folks the defendant was talking
40 to may have been asking directions, and he was merely showing them the
41 way, pointing towards the park or the stores?

1   A. I guess so. But, you know, there are abandoned buildings in that
2 direction too. And very often those are drug drop houses where the corner
3 boys hide their stash.

4   Q. You did not testify whether you searched anywhere down the
5 street, did you?

6   Mr. LEACH: Objection. The question is so vague even I don't know
7 where Ms. Bricker is going.

8   YOUR HONOR: Sustained. Re-ask the question with some param-
9 eters.

10   Ms. BRICKER: Okay. Before or after you arrested the defendant on
11 March 10, YR–00, you did not search any of those abandoned houses on
12 the theory that they were the drug drop house for the defendant, did you?

13   THE WITNESS: Nope. There were just two of us and the defendant
14 could have given us trouble if we tried searching after we arrested him.
15 And beforehand, he could have gotten away.

16   Q. You don't happen to have any idea how many blue stripped
17 Optibikes there are, do you?

18   A. I know that they are darned expensive and that not many folks
19 own them.

20   Q. Would you be surprised if I told you that there are at least ten
21 such bikes registered in the city?

22   A. Are you telling me that?

23   THE COURT: Officer, do I have to warn you again? Answer the ques-
24 tion.

25   THE WITNESS: Again, I am sorry. I would be surprised, I guess, but
26 I am not sure why that would matter.

27   THE COURT: Ah, officer, Alfred Lord Tennyson wrote a poem, yours
28 is not to reason why. That will be for me to decide if this hearing ever
29 ends.

30   Ms. BRICKER: Thank you, Your Honor. I suppose that I will be able
31 to have some input into Your Honor's reasoning!

32   (Laughter).

33   Ms. BRICKER: Officer Giuseppe, thank you. I think that we have
34 taken up enough time for now.

35   THE COURT: Mr. Leach, any re-direct?

36   Mr. LEACH: Just a couple of questions, Your Honor. Actually, skip it.

37   THE COURT: I would like to recess for a few moments. I think that
38 we could all use a cold drink and then get back to business. Mr. Leach,
39 one more witness, is that right?

40   Mr. LEACH: Yes, Your Honor.

41   (After a recess, court is in session).

42   Mr. LEACH: The People call Officer Sid Jones.

43   THE COURT: Would you swear the witness?

1 THE CLERK: Do you solemnly swear that the testimony you are
2 about to give in this case shall be the truth, the whole truth, and nothing
3 but the truth, so help you God?

4 OFFICER JONES: I do.

5 THE CLERK: Please be seated. And would you spell your name for
6 the record?

7 THE WITNESS: S–I–D–N–E–Y J–O–N–E–S.

8 THE COURT: Ready, Mr. Leach?

9   DIRECT EXAMINATION

10 By Mr. LEACH: Officer, for the record, would you state your occupa-
11 tion and how long you have worked in that capacity?

12 THE WITNESS: Well, I am a police officer in the McGeorge City
13 Police Department where I have served since well, since YR–15, January
14 3 of that year. I am in the felony unit now.

15 Q. Let me turn your attention to March 10 of this year. Were you
16 working with Office Giuseppe at that time?

17 A. Not regularly. But on March 10, I was working the narcotics unit.
18 Marla asked me to help her on a case that she was working. She and I
19 went undercover to check out a tip from a CI.

20 Q: A CI? You mean a confidential informant, I assume. Now what
21 happened when you ... well, what happened?

22 A. I see Ms. Bricker ready to stand up. Should I answer?

23 THE COURT: Thank you, Officer. But until she says, "I object," you
24 can continue to testify. Mr. Leach asked a question that probably is too
25 broad but Ms. Bricker isn't wasting our time with technical objections,
26 today.

27 A. OK. So we saw the defendant on the street corner, 5th and Olive.
28 Anybody working narcotics knows that routine. The corner boys signal
29 when a buyer comes by. And that is what we saw. He did it three or four
30 times.

31 Q. Officer, after you saw the defendant signal, you say, three or four
32 times?

33 A. Yes. I think so.

34 Q. What did you do then?

35 A. Well, we started following the defendant on his fancy bike. I
36 knew that it must be stolen. The department thought about getting some
37 of those Optibikes for our bike patrol officers but that would have broken
38 the bank.

39 Q. Did you act just on your suspicion that the bike was stolen?

40 A. No. Marla called into the station and she told me, ...

41 Ms. BRICKER: Objection. That is hearsay.

42 THE COURT: Sustained.

43 Mr. LEACH: May I argue the point?

1   THE COURT: No, Mr. Leach. Find a way to ask the question.

2   Mr. LEACH: Did you stop the defendant?

3   THE WITNESS: Yes.

4   Q. Why did you do so?

5   A. I believed that I had probable cause that the defendant was
6   riding a stolen bike, an expensive one at that. This would have been
7   felony theft.

8   Q. And why did you believe that you had probable cause to arrest?

9   A. Marla, I mean Office Giuseppe told me what she learned from
10   the duty sergeant.

11   THE COURT: Before Ms. Bricker has time to object, overruled. It
12   goes not to the truth, but what the officer believed.

13   Mr. LEACH: So once you stopped the defendant, what did you do?

14   THE WITNESS: I told him that we were police officers, and I showed
15   him my badge. I told him that we were arresting him for theft and that
16   because we were taking him downtown, we had to do a body search.

17   Q. And?

18   A. He had a phone in his shirt pocket. I took it first. It contained a
19   Jitterbug.

20   Q. A what?

21   A. A Jitterbug. That is a cell phone for old people. Big numbers on
22   its keypad. No apps. Simple.

23   Q. Did you continue your search?

24   A. I did. After I took the Jitterbug, I took a pouch that he was hold-
25   ing. I opened that and found a smart phone, an iPhone.

26   Q. Did you continue the search?

27   A. Yes, but that is all that we found on him.

28   Q. What did you do with the bike?

29   A. By this time, a backup unit had arrived, and the officer driving
30   the van was able to put the bike in the van.

31   Q. Did you proceed to take the defendant downtown or did you do
32   anything else first?

33   A. We, I put the defendant in the backseat of our car and hand-
34   cuffed him. Officer Giuseppe drove downtown. And while we were driving,
35   I opened the two phones and looked at them.

36   Q. Why did you do that?

37   A. I was sure that the defendant was a drug dealer, and I wanted to
38   see who he has been calling.

39   Q. What happened then?

40   A. Well, we were back in the station by now. We took the defendant
41   into an interview room after he was booked into the jail.

42   Q. When did you look at the cell phones?

1   A. When he was being booked.

2   Q. What did you find when you looked at the cell phones?

3   A. I jotted down several numbers in his Jitterbug call history sec-
4 tion. And then I opened the iPhone. I opened the messages application
5 and it brought up text conversations. I opened an app; it referred to "TM."

6   Q. What did you find there?

7   A. I found a message sent from one phone number to another and it
8 had a message. It said something like 10100.

9   Q. Wait, before you tell me what that means, walk me through the
10 steps that you took.

11   A. Okay. I had to manipulate the phone; I tapped on an icon, the one
12 that said, messages. That brought up several text message, including the
13 one that I described.

14   Q. How many messages could you see?

15   A. Several.

16   Q. What did those messages mean?

17   Ms. BRICKER: Objection. How does he know?

18   THE COURT: Mr. Leach, how about a foundation?

19   Mr. LEACH: Do you know what the messages meant?

20   THE WITNESS: Yes.

21   Q. How do you know?

22   A. Again, this is part of our narcotics training. We have learned at
23 the academy how drug dealers use numbers, texts to signal what a client
24 wants. Like here, 10100 means ten tablets, probably Vicodin based on the
25 street price, for $100.

26   Q. Did you look at the phones further at this point?

27   A. I did. Well, the iPhone. I saw a directory and saw a file for
28 accounts.

29   Q. How did you know that they were accounts?

30   A. Well, the file was called "accounts." And then he had, like a guy's
31 name, then the amount that he sold him, the kind of drug that he sold.
32 Like one guy, a nickname, "bugsy," "ludes," and the date.

33   Q. Before I hear an objection, would you tell us what "ludes" are
34 and how you know?

35   A. Sure. Ludes is the street name for Quaaludes, which is the brand
36 name for Methaqualone. That was really big before Ecstasy took over
37 with the kids. But some folks still like it. And sure, I know about such
38 drugs because of the training at the academy and then when I served in
39 the narcotics unit.

40   Q. At this point, did you have a conversation with the defendant?

41   A. Well, yes. I told him that he was in trouble, big trouble now.
42 When we'd arrested him, he gave me some lip about how the local D.A.
43 wasn't prosecuting theft anymore because of budget cuts. But when I

1   found evidence that he was a big drug dealer, I told him, big trouble for
2   you. He started to cry and said something like, "I am in big trouble," but
3   I told him to be quiet while I read him his *Miranda* rights.

4   Q.   Slow down. When did you give him his *Miranda* rights?

5   A.   We looked at the phone when he was being booked in. Then we
6   went into the interview room.

7   Q.   And you read him the *Miranda* rights?

8   Ms. BRICKER: Objection, Your Honor. A moment ago the officer tes-
9   tified that he told the suspect that he was in big trouble before he read
10   the defendant his *Miranda* rights. And now, Mr. Leach is suggesting a
11   different scenario to the witness.

12   THE COURT: Officer, what did you say to the defendant before you
13   gave him the *Miranda* rights?

14   THE WITNESS: I, well, let me try to remember exactly what I said.
15   So, I think, like I said, he was giving me some lip and acted like he would
16   just walk out of jail. I told him that we were going to book him in on drug
17   violations because of what we saw on the phone. Then I read him his
18   *Miranda* rights.

19   Mr. LEACH: When you say you gave him his *Miranda* rights, you
20   gave him the rights stated on the card that you carry?

21   A.   Yes. We carry a standard card; it includes the rights as the courts
22   have approved.

23   Ms. BRICKER: Objection, Your Honor. I don't think that Officer
24   Jones is a lawyer qualified to testify about what courts have held.

25   THE COURT: Sustained. Officer, do you have the standard card and
26   the warnings that you gave? I know that counsel is going to want that
27   information.

28   A.   Yes.

29   THE COURT: Mr. Leach, back to you.

30   Mr. LEACH: Officer Jones, you testified that you gave the standard
31   *Miranda* warnings to the defendant. Would you tell us what those warn-
32   ings state?

33   THE WITNESS: Sure. I always use the warnings on the standard
34   issued card. It states, 1. You have the right to remain silent. 2. Anything
35   you say can and will be used against you in a court of law. 3. You have the
36   right to talk to a lawyer and have him present with you while you are
37   being questioned. 4. If you cannot afford to hire a lawyer, one will be
38   appointed to represent you before any questioning. 5. You can decide at
39   any time to exercise these rights and not make any statements or answer
40   any questions.

41   Q.   Did you say anything else?

42   A.   Oh, yes. I then asked the defendant if he understood each of the
43   rights that I just read him.

44   Q.   And, his response?

A. He said that he did. And now, you know, I told him about all of the information that we saw on his cell phones. He admitted his involvement.

Q. Let me back up a second. So you asked if he understood his rights and he said, yes, and then did you ask him if he waived his rights?

Ms. BRICKER: Objection, Your Honor. The officer testified that the suspect spoke up without waiving his rights. And now Mr. Leach seems to want to correct the record.

THE COURT: Mr. Leach, without putting words in the officer's mouth, can you get to the point?

Mr. LEACH: After you read the Miranda warnings, what exactly transpired?

THE WITNESS: Before he finished his answer, I read the rest of what is on the card: you know, "having these rights in mind, do you wish to talk to us now?"

Q. And then the defendant said what?

A. He admitted his involvement in the drug trade. He told us that he was a corner boy. I asked him about the drugs that he had available and, among others, he admitted selling Vicodin.

Mr. LEACH: Nothing further, Your Honor.

THE WITNESS: May I step down now?

THE COURT: No, officer. Ms. Bricker probably has a few questions for you.

Ms. BRICKER: Thank you, Your Honor. You are right about that.

CROSS EXAMINATION

Ms. BRICKER: Morning, Officer. When you took possession of the defendant's Jitterbug, you didn't think that the phone could hurt you in any way, did you?

THE WITNESS: No.

Q. You didn't think that it could contain evidence relating to the theft of the bike, did you?

A. No. I did not.

Q. So once you had the defendant in handcuffs in the backseat of the car, you did not think that he could somehow reach into the front seat and grab the phone, did you?

A. It could happen.

Q. Oh? A handcuffed defendant, in the backseat of the car, with two armed officers in the car, is that realistic?

A. Like I said, it is not impossible.

Q. It has never happened to you, has it? You have never been overpowered by a small person like the defendant, have you?

A. Not me, maybe, but Officer Giuseppe is not as big as I am.

1   Q. So you want us to believe that you thought that the defendant ...
2   uh, let me back up a second. You properly secured the defendant in the
3   backseat, didn't you? He was in handcuffs? You were not careless, were
4   you?

5   A. No. He was secured properly.

6   Q. So then you also got hold of his pouch, didn't you?

7   A. Yes.

8   Q. And you did not fear that it contained a weapon, did you?

9   A. It was big enough to fit a handgun.

10   Q. But you could have felt the pouch and realized that it did not
11   contain a weapon, couldn't you? Mr. Leach did not put that pouch in evi-
12   dence, but is that the pouch over there on counsel's table?

13   A. It is.

14   THE COURT: Well, Mr. Leach, Ms. Bricker, the pouch is not in evi-
15   dence. But I guess that does not matter at this point—neither of you cares
16   about that little technicality. And Ms. Bricker, you are only asking the
17   court to suppress the evidence found on the phone, correct?

18   Ms. BRICKER: Yes, Your Honor. May I continue?

19   THE COURT: Sure.

20   Ms. BRICKER: Back to you, officer. You could feel the pouch and
21   knew that it did not contain a handgun, couldn't you?

22   THE WITNESS: I guess so.

23   Q. And you had the pouch in your possession by the time that the
24   defendant was in the back of the car?

25   A. Yes.

26   Q. You could have put the pouch in the trunk of the car, couldn't
27   you?

28   A. Sure.

29   Q. And you did not think that somehow the defendant could get
30   access to his files on the phone and delete them, did you?

31   A. No.

32   Q. Oh, you didn't think that the pouch contained evidence of bicycle
33   theft, did you?

34   A. No.

35   Q. Oh, I want to go back to the beginning of your testimony. Exactly
36   why did you think that the defendant was involved in drug transactions?

37   A. The neighborhood; his signaling three or four times, telling the
38   people who came up to him where to go to pick up the drugs, signaling
39   someone down the street that a deal was done.

40   Q. So, according to you, anyone living in that neighborhood, or let
41   me start over. You can bust anyone in that neighborhood who happens to
42   make a gesture pointing down the street a couple of times? A grand-
43   mother letting young kids know where they can find a slide and seesaw?

1   A. The defendant is not a grandmother.

2   Q. So any young person would be subject to arrest for such conduct?

3   A. Well, we were acting on the tip too.

4   Q. Anything else?

5   A. Yeah, a fellow officer knew this kid and he was a drug pusher.
6 And we didn't arrest him for drugs anyway. We knew that he stole the
7 bike.

8   Q. So you did not think that you had enough justification to arrest
9 him for drug dealing?

10   Mr. LEACH: Objection. Apart from being argumentative, the officer
11 is not an authority on probable cause.

12   Ms. BRICKER: What?

13   THE COURT: Move on, Ms. Bricker. I get the point, but please move
14 along.

15   Ms. BRICKER: Officer, so when you got the defendant in your car,
16 and you looked at the phones, you told the defendant that he was in big
17 trouble, didn't you?

18   Mr. LEACH: Objection.

19   THE COURT: The basis of your objection is not clear to me, counsel.

20   Mr. LEACH: Well, we have already been over this point. The officer
21 said that he told him that …

22   Ms. BRICKER: Your Honor, Mr. Leach is trying to testify or to remind
23 the officer what he said earlier. Please!

24   THE COURT: I agree. Officer, let me make this simple for all of us:
25 just when did you tell the defendant that he was in big trouble?

26   THE WITNESS: Like I said before, we put the defendant in the inter-
27 view room and before I went in to talk to him, I checked out the phones.
28 When I went in to see him, I thought, you know, the kid had a right to
29 know what he was in there for. He was pretty cocky when he thought that
30 we were just pursuing theft. I did not know if he would want to talk if he
31 knew that we were pursuing drug charges.

32   THE COURT: Back to you, Ms. Bricker. That clears things up a bit,
33 doesn't it?

34   Ms. BRICKER: May we have a sidebar?

35   THE COURT: Let's take a few minutes in my chambers.

36   (The following took place in chambers).

37   THE COURT: Well, Ms. Bricker, you wanted to object to something
38 that I did, I suppose?

39   Ms. BRICKER: Your Honor, I am concerned that your questions made
40 it easy for the officer to figure out the legal issue that I was pursuing. His
41 testimony shows, I think, that he actually engaged in pre-*Miranda* inter-
42 rogation and that the defendant made a response, a partial confession.

43   Mr. LEACH: Your Honor, I would like to say …

1   THE COURT: Mr. Leach, the less said the better. Ms. Bricker, I get
2   the point. I will certainly keep that in mind when I hear arguments.

3   (The following took place in open court).

4   THE COURT: We just had to take care of a little housekeeping. Sorry,
5   Officer. I know that you want to get back to work.

6   Ms. BRICKER: Officer Jones, I want to go back over one more point.
7   I can have Ms. Lester read your testimony back to you if you would like,
8   but I remember you saying that after you read the defendant his rights,
9   he said that he understood his rights and then he immediately admitted
10   his involvement in selling drugs after you told him about what you found
11   on his cell phones, isn't that correct?

12   Mr. LEACH: Objection.

13   THE COURT: Overruled. I have no idea what you are getting at, but
14   I see no possible objection.

15   Ms. BRICKER: Officer?

16   THE WITNESS: I, uh, I think that I said that.

17   Q. So your testimony is that …

18   Mr. LEACH: Objection. This is repetitious.

19   THE COURT: Overruled.

20   Ms. BRICKER: As I was saying, he said that he understood his
21   rights, then you reminded him about finding evidence of his drug activity
22   on his phones, and then he confessed, isn't that what you said earlier and
23   again just now?

24   THE WITNESS: Yes. But he confessed after I finished reading the
25   *Miranda* card. I did ask him if he waived his rights.

26   Q. But as you stated earlier, he admitted his drug involvement
27   without first acknowledging that he waived his rights, isn't that true? Or
28   do you want Ms. Lester to read back your earlier answer?

29   A. No, if you say that is what I said, I am sure that it is.

30   Q. Officer, I … skip it. I am almost done, officer. You have not men-
31   tioned doing an inventory of any evidence found on the defendant, have
32   you?

33   A. No, I have not.

34   Q. And that is because no one thought to do an inventory, isn't that
35   so?

36   A. I don't know what other officers were thinking.

37   Q. I noticed that the People have not charged the defendant with
38   the theft of the bicycle. Do you know why not? And before Mr. Leach
39   object, do you have any personal information why not?

40   A. I don't know.

41   Q. That is it for me.

42   THE COURT: Mr. Leach, I don't see you getting up from counsel
43   table. I assume that means you don't have any re-direct?

1   Mr. LEACH: As always, Your Honor, correct.

2   THE COURT: I have to take a break now. Let's resume at 2:00 when
3   you can make your arguments.

4   (Proceedings concluded).

CHAPTER FIVE

STANDING, CONSENT AND EMERGENCY ENTRANCES

I. INTRODUCTION

The simulation exercise in this chapter gives you an opportunity to explore the rules governing three different doctrines. One is what is often call "standing." The second issue focuses on the validity of a person's consent. The third issue relates to the police's "care-taking function." That is, in some instances, when an officer is not investigating criminal activity, the officer's conduct may be governed by the reasonableness prong of the Fourth Amendment.

This chapter consists of a brief overview of the law governing the three issues described above, a discussion of the role of counsel in this exercise and a transcript of a hearing on the defendant's motion to suppress physical evidence seized from a home where the defendant rented a room.

II. OVERVIEW OF THE LAW

A. "Standing"

Prior to the late 1970's, courts and criminal lawyers asked whether a party who objected to police conduct had standing to object to that conduct. That changed in 1978 in *Rakas v. Illinois,* 439 U.S. 128 (1978), where the Court held that passengers in a vehicle could not object to the search of vehicle absent a showing that they had a reasonable expectation of privacy in the vehicle. Many commentators, including authors of prominent Criminal Procedure casebooks, continue to use the term "standing" because they believe it avoids confusion between two distinct concepts.

As I explain to my students, standing focuses on a person's relationship to the place or property searched or thing seized. The substantive Fourth Amendment issue focuses on police conduct. Analytically, the difference matters: in many cases, the defendant may have standing but the police officers have not violated the Fourth Amendment. In other cases, a defendant may lack standing, even though the police conduct may unquestionably have violated the Fourth Amendment. For example, some of the leading casebooks discuss *United States v. Payner,* 447 U.S. 727 (1980), where the government agents knowingly violated the Fourth Amendment but the government was able to use the evidence against a person who had no interest in the premises searched and no ownership interest in the property seized.

For this exercise, you should consider cases like *Rakas* and some of the post-*Rakas* cases involving homes. In particular, you should focus on *Minnesota v. Olson,* 495 U.S. 91 (1990) and *Minnesota v. Carter,* 525 U.S. 83 (1998). In *Olson,* the Court found that an overnight guest could object to a search of his girlfriend's apartment. In *Carter,* a divided Court held two defendants lacked a sufficient expectation of privacy in an apartment where they were engaged in a drug transaction. In a concurring opinion providing the fifth vote on the standing issue, Justice Kennedy emphasized his view that almost all social guests have a sufficient expectation of privacy to object to searches in their hosts' homes. By contrast, the defendants in *Carter* were in the lessee's apartment briefly and solely for a business purpose. Even this short summary suggests that lower courts have struggled with line drawing between *Olson,* on one hand, and *Rakas* and *Carter* on the other.

B. Consent

(i) Consent to enter the home

The black letter law governing consent is straightforward: the consent must be voluntary. Voluntariness is determined by examining the totality of the circumstances. *Schneckloth v. Bustamonte,* 412 U.S. 218 (1973). No single circumstance is controlling. For example, *Bustamonte* rejected a requirement that the prosecution demonstrate that the defendant knew of his right to refuse to consent. Factors include those relating to the police conduct (e.g., number of police, guns drawn, threats by officers) and to the defendant (e.g., age, gender, race, intelligence, mental condition, level of education, emotional state).

More recently, the Court made clear that when the person giving the consent appears to have authority to consent (i.e., the police reasonably believe the person has authority to consent), the search is lawful. *Illinois v. Rodriguez,* 497 U.S. 177 (1990). As with the voluntariness test, the apparent authority test hardly creates bright lines.

(ii) Consent to enter the defendant's room

Consent cases may involve a second related issue. Even if an initial consent is valid, the police may exceed the scope of that consent. *Florida v. Jimeno,* 500 U.S. 248 (1991) states the black letter law. The legal question focuses on " 'objective' reasonableness." As the Court stated, the question focuses on "what would the typical reasonable person have understood by the exchange between the officer and the suspect?"

C. The Police's Care–Taking Function

At least as long ago as the late 1970's, in *Mincey v. Arizona,* 437 U.S. 385 (1978), the Court recognized police power to enter a home without a warrant when the police are called upon to protect life or prevent an occupant from serious injury. Fourth Amendment protection is greatest when the police seek entry into a home. Typically, the police need probable cause and a warrant, unless the entry comes within a narrow exception. But the police power to enter a home to protect life or to prevent serious injury is not within the police's investigatory function. Instead, the police conduct must be reasonable. *Brigham City v. Stuart,* 547 U.S. 398 (2006). The state carries the burden on proof. *Michigan v. Fisher,* 558 U.S. ___ (2009).

Fisher, a 2009 per curiam opinion, demonstrates that the Court does not want lower courts to engage in too much second-guessing of the police. There, the 7–2 majority rejected the idea that the police must have "ironclad proof" of the need to intervene.

At the same time, the care-taking function exception has outer limits. In *Mincey,* for example, the Court emphasized that once the exigency ended so too did the justification for the police's presence.

As with other issues in this simulation, issues surrounding the care-taking function are fact-sensitive, turning on concepts of reasonableness.

III.   PEOPLE v. MICHAEL KATZ

In this simulation, the People have charged Michael Katz with various drug related offenses.[1] He has moved to suppress the evidence. The trial court conducted an evidentiary hearing to determine the facts relevant to the suppression issue. That transcript appears below.

Your professor will assign a student or students to represent the People and a student or students to serve as defense counsel. Because the court has heard the evidence but not yet made findings of fact, you may argue the facts and, of course, should argue the application of those facts to the law. Without a live witness, you cannot argue credibility based on demeanor. But you can argue whether the witnesses' testimony is credible in light of internal inconsistencies and logic. One lesson you may take from this exercise is that facts are not always as clear as they appear when you read appellate decisions.

More important than factual arguments are the relevant legal arguments. Depending on instructions from your professor, you may argue all of

---

1. Specifically, he has been charged with one count of possession of methaqualone, a Schedule II controlled substance. According to § 111350 of the Pacific Health & Safety Code, "every person who possesses any Schedule II controlled substance shall be punished by imprisonment in the county jail for not more than one year or in state prison." Although the police found the methaqualone in someone else's room, the defendant's fingerprints were found on the bottle. In addition, Mr. Green told the police that the bottle of pills belonged to the defendant.

He has also been charged with one count of possession of cocaine with intent to distribute. Cocaine is a Schedule II controlled substance. According to § 111351 of the Pacific Health & Safety Code, "every person who possesses any Schedule II controlled substance with intent to distribute shall be punished by imprisonment in the state prison for three, six or nine years." The State proves the intent to distribute by showing that the defendant possessed an amount in excess of what one would have for personal use.

the legal issues raised above. You may decide that some of the issues are stronger than others and choose, therefore, to emphasize the strongest arguments that allow you to prevail. Assessing the strength of your legal argument is itself a critical skill that you must learn.

What follows is the transcript of the evidentiary hearing in *People v. Katz.*

1
2   Transcript of the hearing on Defendant Michael Katz's
Motion to Suppress

3   Wednesday, January 6, YR–00

4   The matter of People of the State of Pacific v. Michael Katz, Defen-
5 dant, case number 00–123468, came before the Honorable Michael
6 Vitiello, Judge of the Superior Court of Pacific, County of McGeorge.

7   THE COURT: Call the matter of the People v. Katz. Appearances for
8 the record?

9   MS. CARTER: Leslie Carter for Mr. Katz.

10   MR. MYERS: Jake Myers for the People.

11   THE COURT: Do you both stipulate that there was no warrant?

12   MS. CARTER: Yes.

13   MR. MYERS: Yes.

14   THE COURT: That, of course, shifts the burden to the state. Mr.
15 Myers, are you prepared to call your first witness?

16   MR. MYERS: The People calls Sergeant Hayes.

17   THE COURT: Okay. (The Court administers the oath).

18   TESTIMONY OF ROBERT HAYES

19   DIRECT EXAMINATION

20   MR. MYERS: Sir, how are you employed?

21   A. I am a sergeant with the McGeorge City Police Department. I
22 supervise the narcotics and gang unit.

23   Q. How long have you been a police officer?

24   A. About 23 years.

25   Q. Were you on duty on December 13, YR–01?

26   A. Yes.

27   Q. Did you respond to a call from your dispatcher on that afternoon?

28   A. I did. I heard that a ...

29   MS. CARTER: Objection. He is not answering the question.

30   THE COURT: Sergeant, defense counsel has made a technically cor-
31 rect objection. I know that you are in a hurry to get down to basics, but
32 slowdown and let Mr. Myers ask you a question before you start answer-
33 ing.

34   SERGEANT HAYES: Yes, sir.

35   MR. MYERS: What information did you receive?

36   SERGEANT HAYES: May I refer to my report to refresh my recollec-
37 tion?

38   Q. Yes. Oh, as long as it will refresh your recollection.

39   A. It would. (The witness reviewed his report). Now I remember. The
40 dispatcher told me that a female had been shot and gave me the address

1 and a description of the suspect's vehicle, a 2000 Prius with California
2 license plates.

3   Q. At about what time did you get to the scene?

4   A. About noon.

5   Q What did you see when you arrived at the ... uh, what was the
6 address and when you arrived what did you do at the scene?

7   A. OK, uh, 127 Dry Creek Road. And I saw two young men running
8 down the block. Because I was the first officer on the scene, I did not give
9 chase. And when I arrived at 127 Dry Creek Road, I saw a man, about 35
10 to 40 years old on the porch. He was tending to a young woman, who was
11 bleeding pretty heavily.

12   Q. Who was the man tending to the woman?

13   A. He told me that he was a neighbor and that the woman had been
14 shot by the men who I had seen running down the street.

15   Q. And who was the woman?

16   A. She lived in the house, 127 Dry Creek. Her name is Donna Crane.

17   Q. What was her condition?

18   A. She was agitated, confused. Blood covered her face and was all
19 over her shirt.

20   Q. What did you do then?

21   A. I got a description of the suspects; she identified the two people
22 who were running down the street.

23   Q. At some point, you asked Ms. Crane about entering the residence?

24   A. I did.

25   Q. At that point, did you know who lived there or how many people
26 lived there?

27   A. No.

28   Q. Were you concerned about Ms. Crane?

29   A. Yes. She seemed disoriented and had lost blood.

30   Q. Did you ask her how many people were in the house?

31   A. Yes, but she did not answer. I had to ask her the question three
32 times.

33   Q. Did she ever answer you?

34   A. She did.

35   Q. And?

36   A. She said that she did not believe that anyone was in the house.

37   Q. Were you satisfied with her answer?

38   A. Absolutely not.

39   Q. Why not?

40   A. She seemed confused. She had a serious head injury and did not
41 seem to fully understand me.

1 Q. Why were you concerned about whether someone was in the
2 home?

3 A. I still didn't know whose house it was. Then I thought, the report
4 was that suspects fled in a Prius and then I saw two suspects running
5 down the street. This could be a gang hit, and I was worried that other
6 people could be in the house.

7 Q. And you were concerned ... let me start over. Were you concerned
8 about officer safety because you were on the porch where a shooting had
9 just taken place?

10 A. Of course. And a backup unit was heading into the area, and I
11 didn't want us to walk into an ambush.

12 Q. In your experience, do people in Ms. Crane's situation give accu-
13 rate information?

14 MS. CARTER: Objection. That is pure speculation, and we have no
15 idea how often the sergeant has responded to such situations.

16 THE COURT: Sustained.

17 MR. MYERS: Did you have any reason to doubt Ms. Crane's reliabil-
18 ity?

19 A. Yes. She was completely disoriented.

20 Q. Did you ask Ms. Crane to let you in the house?

21 A. Yes.

22 Q. Did she open the door and agree to let you in?

23 A. No. Again, I am not sure if she understood my question.

24 Q. At some point, you decided to enter?

25 A. I did. As I explained, I was worried about other victims and the
26 other officers who had just arrived at the scene.

27 Q. How did you gain entry?

28 A. I told Ms. Crane that I really needed the key to the house and that
29 I did not want to damage the door frame.

30 Q. How did she respond?

31 A. She handed me the key and said, "go ahead."

32 Q. Did you enter?

33 A. No.

34 Q. Why not?

35 A. I did not have on protective gear, like the backup unit which had
36 shown up.

37 Q. I take it that you were concerned about officers having safety
38 equipment because they could face resistance in the home?

39 A. Yes. Obviously, someone had been shot here and someone or other
40 people could still be inside, either injured or wanting to harm an officer.

41 MR. MYERS: Thank you.

1   CROSS EXAMINATION

2   MS. CARTER: Sergeant, when you got the call originally, what crime
3   did you think that you were investigating?

4   A. A shooting. A potential homicide.

5   Q. How many victims?

6   A. I don't remember.

7   Q. Your information did not indicate more than one victim?

8   A. Not that I recall, but it may have.

9   Q. You say, "may have," but you did testify just now that you don't
10 remember, isn't that correct?

11   A. Yes. But I remember being concerned that other victims may have
12 been in the house based on all of my observations.

13   Q. Once you were at the scene, surely you would have tried to cor-
14 roborate information about the Prius, wouldn't you?

15   A. Of course, and I did.

16   Q. Oh? How?

17   A. I asked Ms. Crane.

18   Q. And she told you that she had seen a Prius flee from the scene,
19 didn't she?

20   A. Uh, yes, I think so.

21   Q. So you are telling me that she was lucid enough to describe the
22 people who fled from the scene?

23   A. I guess so.

24   Q. Did you check to see what was causing Ms. Crane's bleeding?

25   A. Uh, …

26   Q. You were concerned for her safety, weren't you?

27   A. Of course.

28   Q. Did you notice that her wounds were consistent with a gunshot
29 wound? That was the source of her injuries, wasn't it?

30   A. Uh, I …

31   Q. Didn't the neighbor tell you that she had been shot?

32   A. As far as I can recall, I guess so.

33   Q. Nothing further. Oh, Your Honor, may I ask two more questions?

34   THE COURT: Yes.

35   MS. CARTER: Did you discuss this case with Mr. Myers before your
36 testimony today?

37   A. Yes.

38   Q. Did he tell you what defense counsel was arguing?

39   A. No.

1   Q. Did Mr. Myers tell you about the rules allowing police to enter to
2   search for victims of a crime and the police's ability to do protective
3   sweeps of houses?

4   A. No. That is part of our routine police training.

5   THE COURT: Ms. Carter, I thought that you said two more ques-
6   tions? You are up to three already. Are you almost done?

7   MS. CARTER: Yes, but please indulge me for a minute.

8   THE COURT: Sure.

9   MS. CARTER: Ms. Crane did tell you that no one else was in the
10   home, didn't she?

11   A. Yes. But I saw blood on the door and from what I could tell, the
12   blood went inside too.

13   Q. Well, wait, what could you see in the residence, there wasn't a
14   window open or a window in the door or anything like that was there? I
15   didn't see anything like that in the crime scene photo—was I missing
16   something?

17   MR. MYERS: Objection, Your Honor. Apart from testifying, Ms.
18   Carter is throwing a whole lot of questions at the sergeant.

19   THE COURT: Sergeant, first, could you see in the house through a
20   window or otherwise?

21   A. No. The blinds were closed, but I did see some blood around the
22   door frame.

23   MS. CARTER: You didn't hear noises coming from inside the house,
24   did you?

25   A. Not that I remember, but things were moving fast and my strong
26   impressions were that something was wrong here.

27   Q. Back to how you gained entry, you don't really think that Ms.
28   Crane consented to the entry when she responded to your threat to break
29   in the door?

30   A. I was not threatening her, and I was just telling her what the law
31   lets me do. I mean may even require me to do because someone may have
32   been lying injured in the house.

33   Q. Oh? Withdraw the question. Well, I am a little confused, Sergeant.
34   You tell me that you had a long conversation with Ms. Crane but that you
35   thought that she was too confused to trust her answer about whether
36   anyone was in the house. How can it be that you listened to her for a long
37   time, seemed interested in the information that she gave you?

38   A. I started to distrust her; her responses were somewhat untruthful
39   and that raised my suspicions.

40   Q. Suspicions? You mean that you suspected that she might be
41   involved in criminal activity, don't you?

42   MR. MYERS: Objection.

43   THE COURT: The basis of your objection, Mr. Myers?

44   MR. MYERS: Argumentative. And Ms. Carter is distorting what the
45   witness is saying. He indicated that he was worried about other shooting

1 victims. Ms. Carter is trying to make it sound like he believed that Ms.
2 Crane was involved in criminal activity.

3 THE COURT: Overruled.

4 MS. CARTER: Sergeant, back to my question. You thought that
5 criminal activity was taking place inside, didn't you?

6 A. No. I still thought that someone might have been shot.

7 Q. Well, can you point to any objective facts that would lead to that
8 conclusion?

9 A. I told you before. Ms. Crane was not being truthful with me. She
10 was evasive in her answers. And she was disoriented.

11 Q. Have you ever met Ms. Crane before?

12 A. No.

13 Q. So you have no basis on which to tell if she is truthful or not, other
14 than the fact that she had been injured and may have been a little con-
15 fused?

16 A. Well, there was blood on the door.

17 THE COURT: Ms. Carter, aren't we going around the block again
18 here? And you told me ten minutes ago that you had only two questions.

19 MS. CARTER: I am almost done, Your Honor. Promise.

20 Q. Apart from concern about victims, you thought that there might be
21 some evidence of illegal activity in the house?

22 A. At that particular time, no. I really was concerned about other vic-
23 tims, primarily, and then maybe a hidden gunman.

24 Q. But you told me that the dispatcher reported two suspected gun-
25 men and you saw them running down the street, didn't you?

26 A. This could have been a gang crime. I saw the two men running and
27 knew that a couple of others had been in the Prius.

28 Q. A gang crime, like a drug-related hit, isn't that correct?

29 A. Maybe.

30 Q. Back to the beginning, you did respond to a call from the dis-
31 patcher that someone had been shot, didn't you?

32 A. Yes.

33 Q. And when you got to the scene, you saw someone who had been
34 shot?

35 A. Yes, I did.

36 THE COURT: Ms. Carter?

37 MS. CARTER: Your Honor, that's it for me. Thank you for indulging
38 me.

39 THE COURT: Mr. Myers, any redirect? It is getting late in the day,
40 and I am sure that you have more witnesses or at least one more witness.

41 MR. MYERS: Your Honor, just a couple of questions.

42 THE COURT: As you wish.

1   MR. MYERS: Sergeant, didn't the dispatcher tell you that someone
2   reported a possible home entry at 127 Dry Creek Road?

3   A. Oh, yes, the dispatcher did tell me that.

4   Q. And when you got there, how would you describe the conditions,
5   with Ms. Crane bleeding and having trouble focusing? Chaotic?

6   MS. CARTER: Objection, Your Honor. Mr. Myers is leading and is
7   testifying as well.

8   THE COURT: Sustained.

9   MR. MYERS: Sergeant, please describe the scene when you arrived
10   so that we have an idea of how quickly you had to make your decision.

11   MS. CARTER: Objection.

12   THE COURT: Overruled.

13   MR. MYERS: Sergeant, you may answer the question unless you
14   need the court reporter to read it back?

15   A. The scene was chaotic. I got there, Ms. Crane was bleeding; I was
16   worried about the potential victims in the house and worried that I would
17   be sending in the backup unit team members into hostile fire.

18   MR. MYERS: Nothing more, Your Honor. The People call ...

19   MS. CARTER: Your Honor, I am entitled to re-cross.

20   THE COURT: I did not think that you had more questions, but, of
21   course, you are right.

22   MS. CARTER: Sergeant, you did not see any evidence of a forced
23   entry, did you?

24   A. No.

25   Q. Nothing more, Your Honor.

26   THE COURT: Thank you, Ms. Carter. Now back to you, Mr. Myers.

27   MR. MYERS: The People call Officer David Cheng.

28   (Witness Officer David Cheng takes the stand and is sworn in.)

29   MR. MYERS: Can you tell me your background, who employs you
30   and how long you have worked for that employer?

31   OFFICER CHENG: For the past twelve years, I have been employed
32   as a police officer with the McGeorge City Police Department.

33   Q. On December 13 YR–01, were you working in that capacity?

34   A. Yes.

35   Q. Can you describe whether at some point you responded to a call of
36   a situation at 127 Dry Creek Road in McGeorge?

37   A. I did.

38   Q. At about what time?

39   A. I arrived at the scene at around 12:20 or 12:30.

40   Q. Would you describe the scene when you arrived?

1   A. Sergeant Hayes was at the scene, and he was engaged with a
2   woman. I could see immediately she was bleeding and he was trying to
3   take care of her.

4   Q. Was he the only officer on the scene?

5   A. Yes.

6   Q. Were you alone?

7   A. No, I arrived with my partner. Another Black and White arrived a
8   few minutes later.

9   Q. Were you in uniform?

10   A. Yes, and I was wearing a protective vest, as was my partner and
11 the other officers who arrived at the same time.

12   Q. At some point, do you recall receiving instructions to enter the
13 home?

14   A. Yes. Sergeant Hayes told me that …

15   MS. CARTER: Objection, this obviously gets into hearsay.

16   MR. MYERS: But this goes to state of mind.

17   THE COURT: Mr. Myers is obviously correct. Overruled.

18   MR. MYERS: What was your understanding why you were making
19 the entry?

20   A. To make sure that no one else was in the house, someone injured
21 or maybe another shooter.

22   Q. When you entered, uh, back up a second. Was the door open when
23 you entered?

24   A. Yes. Well, I saw the Sergeant unlock the door with the key that the
25 victim gave him.

26   Q. Did you make the entry alone?

27   A. No.

28   Q. Who made the entry with you?

29   A. My partner, Officer Jim Parker.

30   Q. When you entered, where did you go first?

31   Q. Well, it looked like a dining room. There was a big table there.

32   A. So, uh, was there an upstairs?

33   Q. Yes.

34   A. So how did you proceed in sweeping through the house?

35   MS. CARTER: Objection.

36   THE COURT: The basis of your objection?

37   MS. CARTER: May I have a sidebar, Your Honor?

38   THE COURT: Yes.

39   (Side bar)

1   MS. CARTER: Mr. Myers has not established whether this was a
2 sweep through the house or a full search. He is planting in the officer's
3 mind the idea that this was a protective sweep and it may have been a
4 search for evidence without any legal basis.

5   MR. MYERS: I resent the suggestion that I am doing something
6 improper.

7   MS. CARTER: I did not say that you were aware of what you are
8 doing.

9   THE COURT: Enough. This is not a school yard. The objection is
10 granted.

11   MR. MYERS: Officer, how did you proceed once you were in the
12 house?

13   A. Well, we looked around the dining room and a living room and the
14 kitchen, quickly sweeping through the house to see if anyone else was
15 there.

16   Q. Did anything catch your attention when you were downstairs?

17   A. No. It was messy.

18   Q. At some point, you went upstairs to continue your sweep? Uh, I
19 mean to continue looking around?

20   A. Yes.

21   Q. Describe where you were looking upstairs.

22   A. Bedrooms and the bathroom. I did see a bottle of pills in one of the
23 bedrooms that looked suspicious.

24   Q. Like what?

25   A. It could have been methaqualone.

26   Q. Was the bottle in the defendant's room?

27   A. No.

28   Q. Did you seize the bottle at that point?

29   A. No.

30   Q. Why not?

31   A. I was looking to see if anyone was on the second floor.

32   Q. Were you looking in cupboards or drawers?

33   A. No.

34   Q. Why not?

35   A. As I said, I was looking to see if anyone was there. Or if a body was
36 there.

37   Q. Did you enter all of the rooms upstairs?

38   A. Not right away.

39   Q. Why not?

40   A. One of the bedrooms was locked.

41   Q. Why didn't you enter right away?

1   A. I didn't want to damage the property.

2   Q. What did you do?

3   A. I went back downstairs and asked the Sergeant whether he had
4   the key to the room.

5   Q. And?

6   A. He told me that he didn't and that I should break in the door.

7   Q. Which you did?

8   A. Yes.

9   Q. What did you find there?

10   A. Evidence of cocaine.

11   Q. Specifically?

12   A. There was a large amount of cocaine, some in a bag, some in small
13   baggies. There was a desk in the room and a scale was on top of the desk.

14   Q. How did you know that this was cocaine?

15   A. Uh, what do you mean? It was cocaine.

16   Q. In your years as an officer, have you had any training in recogniz-
17   ing cocaine?

18   A. Oh. Yes. On the job training and at the academy.

19   Q. What did you do then?

20   A. I seized the cocaine, the scales, and baggies. I also went back
21   downstairs and grabbed the bottle of pills.

22   Q. Do you have any idea who used that room?

23   A. Yes.

24   Q. Who and how did you know?

25   A. After I loaded up the contraband, a man identified himself as the
26   owner of the house.

27   Q. Who is that?

28   A. He said his name was Leon Green.

29   Q. And he told you that the room was whose?

30   A. He said that the defendant Michael Katz rented the room and that
31   he, Green, had no idea what Katz did in the room.

32   Q. I have no further questions.

33   CROSS EXAMINATION

34   MS. CARTER: Ok, so officer, did you hear a conversation between the
35   sergeant and Ms. Crane when she gave him the key?

36   A. Yes.

37   Q. The sergeant did tell Ms. Crane that he would knock down the
38   door if she did not provide the key?

39   A. Yes, he seemed upset that we could not respond …

1   MS. CARTER: Your Honor, please instruct the witness to answer the
2   question.

3   THE COURT: Ms. Carter, you opened the door, well, so to speak. But
4   officer, please try to limit your answers to the lawyers' questions.

5   A. Ok. So what is the question?

6   MS. CARTER: Once the door was open, you went into what you
7   described as the dining area, correct?

8   A. Yes.

9   Q. You testified a moment ago that the room where you entered
10   looked like a dining room. Anything exceptional about the room?

11   A. I am not sure that I understand the question.

12   Q. Did you see anything out of the ordinary in the room?

13   A. No. It had a big table and some chairs.

14   Q. But you have not testified as to any blood or as to any furniture
15   overturned, or any other sign of struggle, have you?

16   A. No.

17   Q. Why not?

18   A. Because there was none.

19   Q. Oh, I forgot to ask you, when you entered the house, did you
20   announce your presence?

21   A. Yes.

22   Q. Did anyone respond?

23   A. No.

24   Q. Did you hear any sounds, anyone in distress?

25   A. No.

26   Q. So when you went upstairs and got to the locked bedroom, did you
27   knock on the door?

28   A. I believe so.

29   Q. I thought that you said that you ran downstairs to ask the ser-
30   geant what to do?

31   A. That was after I knocked on the door.

32   Q. Did anyone respond when you knocked on the door?

33   A. No.

34   MS. CARTER: I have nothing further, Your Honor.

35   REDIRECT EXAMINATION

36   MR. MYERS: Officer, you said in response to Ms. Carter's question
37   that you did not see any blood in the residence. But were you looking for
38   blood?

39   A. Oh, no, not at all. I was worried about finding other victims and
40   watching out for the perpetrator.

1
2
Q. And would you have been engaging in a careful search for blood or would you be just taking a quick look around?

3
4
A. Just a glance. In that kind of situation, you just don't have time to do more than glance.

5
Q. Were you supposed to process the crime scene?

6
A. No, that was not my job.

7
MR. MYERS: Nothing further Your Honor.

8
9
10
MS. CARTER: Just a couple of questions. Officer, you were suspicious that Ms. Crane was hiding something when she refused entry, weren't you?

11
A. Yes.

12
Q. Anything specific?

13
14
A. The neighborhood is a high crime area and some people in the area sell drugs.

15
MS. CARTER: Nothing further.

16
THE COURT: Mr. Myers, any additional witnesses?

17
MR. MYERS: One more, Your Honor. The People call Leon Green.

18
(Witness Leon Green takes the stand and is sworn in).

19
DIRECT EXAMINATION

20
MR. MYERS: State your full name and address for the record.

21
22
LEON GREEN: Leon Green, 127 Dry Creek Road, McGeorge City, State of Pacific.

23
Q. Do you own that home?

24
A. Yes.

25
Q. Who else lives there?

26
27
A. Donna Crane and her boyfriend, Larry Leavitt, rent from me. They share the master bedroom upstairs and have use of the rest of the house.

28
Q. What about Michael Katz, does he live there?

29
A. No.

30
31
32
Q. Are you aware that narcotics were found in a room, uh, let me begin again. Did you tell a police officer that Katz rented the room where narcotics were found during a search on December 13 of last year?

33
34
35
A. Oh, yes. A month earlier, Katz asked me if he could rent a room from me for a month or two. He did not sleep there. He wanted to use it to store stuff.

36
Q. What kind of stuff?

37
A. Hey, don't ask, don't tell. I did not care. I needed the rent money.

38
Q. Did you know what was in his room?

39
A. No. He insisted on having a lock on the door.

40
Q. How often did Mr. Katz use the room?

1   A. I don't know. Not often.

2   Q. Did he ever spend the night in the room?

3   A. No. It was not set up with a bed as far as I knew.

4   Q. Did people come to the house to see him?

5   A. No.

6   MR. MYERS: Nothing further Your Honor.

7   CROSS EXAMINATION

8   MS. CARTER: Could Mr. Katz have slept in his room, had he chosen
9   to do so?

10   A. I guess so.

11   Q. Well, you had no agreement that he could not do so, did you?

12   A. No.

13   Q. When you said that he never spent the night in the room, you are
14   not sure, are you?

15   A. No. I was out of town on occasion and did not check to see if he did.
16   But he did not have a bed, as far as I knew.

17   Q. How much did he pay you for the use of the room?

18   MR. MYERS: Objection. Relevance.

19   THE COURT: Ms. Carter, does it make a difference? The day is
20   almost over. Do we really need a lot more information from this witness?

21   MS. CARTER: Your Honor, Mr. Myers is about to tell you that Mr.
22   Katz lacks standing to object to an illegal search. I want to show the level
23   of, uh, the extent of Mr. Katz's relationship to the premises.

24   THE COURT: Overruled. Mr. Green, answer the question, if you
25   remember it.

26   A. Yes. How much rent did Katz pay? He paid me $350 for three
27   month's use of the room.

28   THE COURT: Ms. Carter, anything else?

29   MS. CARTER: Nothing else, Your Honor.

30   THE COURT: Mr. Myers, do you need redirect?

31   MR. MYERS: No, Your Honor. The People rest.

32   THE COURT: Given the lateness of the hour, we are going to adjourn
33   for the day. I have an opening in my calendar for tomorrow at 10:00 A.M.
34   Are you both available to argue this motion at that time?

35   MR. MYERS: Yes, Your Honor. I will be here bright and early.

36   THE COURT: Thank you, Mr. Myers. As usual, you are helpful to the
37   court. Ms. Carter, how about you?

38   MS. CARTER: Is it possible to begin at 10:30? I have a commitment
39   in Judge Caplan's courtroom at 9:00 and I don't want to keep you waiting
40   if it runs late.

41   THE COURT: Well, I suppose so. 10:30, sharp, no excuses.

CHAPTER SIX

SPECIAL NEEDS AND THE FOURTH AMENDMENT

I. INTRODUCTION

The simulation exercise in this chapter gives you an opportunity to explore the rules governing the Court's special needs doctrine. It entails one primary issue. In various settings, the Court has held the ordinary Fourth Amendment rules do not apply. When police officers are not engaged in criminal investigations, Fourth Amendment requirements of probable cause and warrants ordinarily do not apply. In recent years, the Court has described these cases as ones involving "special needs." As developed below, the Court has found that in some cases, "special needs, beyond the normal needs of law enforcement, make the warrant and probable-cause requirement impracticable." *Griffin v. Wisconsin,* 483 U.S. 868 (1987). If a court concludes the police conduct comes within this doctrine, the police or other state actors may not have to demonstrate any level of suspicion to engage in conduct that amounts to a search or seizure. As a result, a threshold question in such cases is whether the case comes within the traditional rules under the Fourth Amendment or whether it comes within the special needs doctrine.

II. OVERVIEW OF THE LAW

Imagine a public school student who is called into her principal's office on suspicion that she has been smoking in violation of school rules. If the Fourth Amendment requirements of probable cause and a search warrant applied (absent a narrow exception), the principal would not be able to demand access to the student's purse to see if she had cigarettes if the principal could not meet the traditional Fourth Amendment requirements. But such a case looks different from an ordinary criminal investigation. After all, school officials need to be able to maintain discipline, and at least at the outset, the goal of the search is disciplinary, not criminal.

Or think about the extraordinarily invasive searches of airline passengers and their luggage. In such cases, state actors engage in searches with no individualized suspicion. Absent reliance on a questionable consent theory, such searches would be impossible if traditional Fourth Amendment requirements applied.

Enter the special needs doctrine. Although the Court did not coin the term "special needs" until the 1980s, the doctrine traces its origins to the late 1960s. In *Camara v. Municipal Court,* 387 U.S. 523 (1967), the Court held local officials could conduct a safety inspection without a homeowner's consent based on a warrant issued on less than the usual level of probable cause. The Court introduced a balancing test that focused on a number of factors, including the judicial history and public acceptance of a police practice, the need to achieve acceptable results that would be frustrated by the traditional requirements of the Fourth Amendment, and the degree of intrusion of the practice the state attempted to justify. *Camara's* balancing test has worked its way into the Court's Fourth Amendment law, especially in cases involving special needs.[1]

Commentators view *New York v. Burger*, 482 U.S. 691 (1987), as the outer limit of the Court's special needs cases. Two earlier Court cases found that various kinds of businesses have been subject to a long history of regulation. Read together, *Colonnade Catering Corp. v. United States,* 397 U.S. 72 (1970), and *United States v. Biswell,* 406 U.S. 311 (1972), established special rules involving inspections of regulated businesses. Regulators are able to search business premises without warrants if inspections are crucial to the regulatory scheme; the negligible protection of a warrant would frustrate the inspections that need to be unannounced and frequent, and the inspections pose limited interference with the business owner's justifiable expectations of privacy.

At issue in *Burger* was the lawfulness of a warrantless search of an automobile junkyard. New York enacted a statute aimed at regulating such facilities because they had become part of a lucrative auto theft market, whereby junk dealers could strip stolen cars and sell used parts. Despite the fact that the "inspectors" were police officers and the goal of the regulatory scheme was to investigate crime, the Court balanced the *Biswell* factors and concluded that the New York statute did not violate the Fourth Amendment.

This simulation focuses on an issue not yet resolved by the Court. Many states have in place statutes authorizing conservation officers to search fishermen or hunters even though the officers lack probable cause to believe that the fishermen or hunters have violated fish and game regulations. Some of those statutes authorize conservation officers to stop fishermen or hunters and demand to see what they have caught without a showing of any level of suspicion. Lower courts have divided on how those cases should be resolved. That is the subject of this simulation.

III. PEOPLE v. JOHN SKATE PIKE

On June 20, YR–01, Pacific Fish and Game Warden Tony Mola was patrolling in the northern part of the State of Pacific. His special concern was

---

1. The Court has used the balancing approach in numerous traditional Fourth Amendment cases. One of the earliest cases was *Terry v. Ohio*, 392 U.S. 1 (1968), which allowed police to engage in a brief detention and patdown based on a lesser showing of suspicion than probable cause. As you have studied or will study in your course, Chief Justice Warren envisioned *Terry* as a limited exception to traditional Fourth Amendment requirements. However, the Court has extended *Terry* well beyond the original limited context of street confrontations between police and criminal suspects.

Coho Salmon, an endangered species that was once abundant in the streams of northern Pacific. He was responsible for covering many hundreds of square miles, especially in light of recent budget cuts. An experienced warden, he was aware that Pacific Fish and Wildlife regulations authorized him to detain anyone who was fishing or hunting and to inspect that person's automobile or containers that might hold fish or wildlife.

While on patrol, Mola saw a man, later identified as John Skate Pike, exit the woods. Pike had parked in a lot that had access to a stream where Coho salmon could still be found. Mola noticed Pike dragging a heavy ice chest, commonly used by fishermen to pack beer and keep their catch. As developed at the hearing, Mola asked Pike whether Pike had a fishing license (he did) and whether he had been fishing (he had). Mola then demanded to see the contents of Pike's ice chest. Not only did Mola find two large salmon, he also found a sizeable amount of marijuana in the ice chest.

Authorized to arrest criminal suspects, not just to cite misdemeanants, Mola arrested Pike. Pike has been charged with possession of marijuana with intent to distribute. Pike's attorney has filed a motion to suppress the evidence.

In the
SUPERIOR COURT
FOR THE COUNTY OF BRAINERD

State of Pacific
Plaintiff

Criminal Action No. 00–156JD

vs.

Judge: John Foss

Defendant John Skate Pike

I. Defendant's Motion to Suppress

Defendant, being a person aggrieved by an unlawful arrest, search and seizure, moves to suppress for use as evidence all items obtained by said arrest, search and seizure and all other evidence obtained as a result thereof on the following grounds:

1. On June 20, YR–01, the Defendant was arrested by a Pacific Fish and Game Warden.

2. The game warden lacked any suspicion that the Defendant was engaged in criminal activity or had violated any fish or wildlife regulations.

3. Despite the absence of any kind of suspicion, no less probable cause, the game warden detained the Defendant.

4. Despite the absence of any kind of suspicion, the game warden demanded that the Defendant open his ice chest, where the game warden found and seized marijuana.

5. For the above reasons and otherwise, the Defendant's arrest was in violation of his Fourth Amendment rights to be free from unreasonable searches and seizures.

6. The Defendant urges this court to suppress the fruits of his illegal arrest and the illegal search of his property.

Dated: August 5, YR–01

Respectfully submitted,

Anne Kramer

Anne Kramer
Attorney-at-Law
123 Main Square
Brainerd, Pacific 95715
Telephone: (549) 555–5100

Attorney for Defendant John Skate Pike

In the
SUPERIOR COURT
FOR THE COUNTY OF BRAINERD

State of Pacific
Plaintiff

Criminal Action No. 00–156JD

vs.

Judge: John Foss

Defendant John Skate Pike

Memorandum of Points and Authorities on Behalf of Defendant

I. Introduction

John Skate Pike has been charged with the unlawful possession of ten pounds of marijuana with intent to distribute.

II. Facts

On June 20, YR–01, a Pacific fish and game warden saw Mr. Pike leaving a path that led from a stream. He observed Mr. Pike carrying an ice chest. The game warden first asked Mr. Pike if he had a fishing license. He said, truthfully, that he did have a license. The game warden then asked him if he had been fishing. Again, truthfully, Mr. Pike said that he had been. Thereafter, the game warden insisted on seeing the contents of Mr. Pike's ice chest. When the game warden discovered marijuana, he arrested Mr. Pike for possession of marijuana with intent to distribute.

Thereafter, Mr. Pike was indicted for possession of marijuana with intent to distribute.

III. Argument

The Fourth Amendment protects against unreasonable searches and seizures. Consistent with the Fourth Amendment, the Supreme Court has held repeatedly that the police must have probable cause and a warrant to search, subject to a limited number of narrow exceptions. The facts of the instant case do not come within any recognized exceptions.

In the instant case, the game warden was acting under Pacific Fish and Game regulations that allow stops, searches and seizures based on no justification at all. This statute is a clear violation of the Fourth Amendment.

IV. Conclusion

For the foregoing reasons, Mr. Pike requests the court to suppress all of the evidence obtained as a result of the violation of his Fourth Amendment rights.

Respectfully submitted,

Anne Kramer

Anne Kramer

Attorney at Law
123 Main Square
Brainerd, Pacific 95715
Telephone: (549) 555–5100
Attorney for Defendant John Skate
Pike

Transcript of the hearing on Defendant John S. Pike's
Motion to Suppress

Friday, September 18, YR–00

The matter of People of the State of Pacific v. John Skate Pike, Defendant, case number 00–156JD, came before the Honorable John Foss, Judge of the Superior Court of Pacific, County of Brainerd.

THE COURT: Good morning, ladies and gentlemen. Okay. For the record, this is People of the State of Pacific v. John Skate Pike. Enter your appearances for the record.

MS. MATHER: Caryn Mather for the People of Pacific, Your Honor.

MS. KRAMER: Anne Kramer for the Defendant, Mr. John Skate Pike.

THE COURT: Good to see you both. Ms. Kramer, I have read your papers. I imagine that I am going to need some post-hearing briefing as well. Based on some quick research, I believe that the question is a close one.

MS. KRAMER: Of course, Your Honor.

THE COURT: Thank you for your cooperation. Now, absent a warrant, Ms. Mather, the ball is in your court. Are you ready to call your witness or witnesses?

MS. MATHER: Yes, Your Honor. The People have only one witness. The People call Mr. Anthony Mola.

Warden Anthony Mola was called as a witness, being duly sworn, was examined and testified as follows:

DIRECT EXAMINATION

MS. MATHER: Warden, would you please state your name for the court and spell your name for the court reporter?

A.   Anthony Michael Mola. Mola is M–O–L–A.

MS. MATHER: What is your official position?

A.   I am a Fish and Game Warden with the State of Pacific.

MS. MATHER: How long have you held that position?

A.   This is my fifteenth year.

MS. MATHER: Thank you, warden. Now I want to go back to June 20 of last year. Were you on duty at that time?

A.   Yes. I was patrolling in northern Pacific, around Fort Brainerd. We have a lot of trouble in that area with folks taking Coho Salmon.

MS. MATHER: Okay. So, oh, I am sorry. I did not mean to interrupt. Continue explaining your concerns about that area.

A.   Sure. That area of the state has a lot of outdoorsmen and outdoorswomen. A lot of them resent government ...

MS. KRAMER: Objection, Your Honor. On what does the warden base these stereotypes?

1   THE COURT: Nice point, Ms. Kramer. Ms. Mather, if your view is
2 that the warden is competent to testify on this matter, how about quali-
3 fying him?

4   MS. MATHER: Of course, Your Honor. Warden, in your experience,
5 well, first, so that Ms. Kramer does not have to object again, during your
6 fifteen years experience as a game warden for the State of Pacific, have
7 you spent much time in the Brainerd area?

8   A.   I certainly have. I have been assigned that area and similar
9 areas for years, probably ten years.

10   Q.   So are you familiar with local residents in the Brainerd area?

11   A.   I am. I often run into them in the woods and then in town, at the
12 coffee shop there.

13   Q.   And when you run into them, as you say, have you discussed
14 their views of environmental protection regulations, like the laws that
15 you are sworn to enforce?

16   A.   I do.

17   Q.   And what is the view of folks in the Brainerd area? Are they
18 generally supportive of government and governmental regulations?

19   A.   No, they are not. A lot of them think that government is a bad
20 thing and that they can do a better job than some bureaucrat in Washing-
21 ton or in McGeorge City.

22   Q.   So back to June 20, if you would.

23   A.   I was on duty, and I pulled into a parking area that leads to a
24 stream where we are still fortunate to have some Coho Salmon now and
25 then. We have had plenty of bad experiences there because locals like to
26 take Coho—you know why; that is one of the best eating salmon out
27 there.

28   Q.   And so on the 20th, what happened?

29   A.   I pulled into the parking lot, and shortly after I got there, I saw
30 a guy dragging a heavy ice chest. Usually, when fishermen leave that
31 area, they have drunk all of their beer and they don't have to drag their
32 ice chests. That is the case unless they have a chest full of fish. So I fig-
33 ured this guy was over the limit.

34   Q.   What happened after you saw him, oh, by the way, who was the
35 person dragging the chest?

36   A.   The defendant, John Pike.

37   Q.   Is he in the courtroom today?

38   A.   Yes. (Pointing) He's the guy over there, next to Ms. Kramer.

39   Q.   So you saw him and what happened?

40   A.   Well, I went up to him and asked him if he had a license. He
41 showed me his license. Then I asked if he had been fishing and he said,
42 yes. At that point, I told him that I wanted to see what was in his ice
43 chest.

44   Q.   Did he consent to the search?

1   A.   Well, not exactly.

2   Q.   What do you mean?

3   A.   He told me to go F* * * myself.

4   Q.   Oh. What did you do in response to that comment?

5   A.   I told him that I was going to look in his ice chest.

6   Q.   Were you at all concerned about your safety?

7   A.   Yes. So I put my hand on my pistol, to remind him that it was
8 there. I told him to back up and not to move.

9   Q.   Did he comply?

10   A.   After he seemed to look around—I think he was looking to see if
11 he could run away.

12   MS. KRAMER: Objection. That is pure speculation.

13   THE COURT: Sustained.

14   MS. MATHER: Apart from speculating about the defendant's plans,
15 what did he do?

16   A.   He stood there while I flipped open his ice chest. And ...

17   Q.   And?

18   A.   Voila! Two fat Coho and what I recognized immediately as mari-
19 juana.

20   Q.   How did you know that it was marijuana?

21   A.   I have received training in the police academy. We studied drug
22 identification.

23   Q.   What did you do once you recognized that he possessed mari-
24 juana?

25   A.   I told him that he was under arrest. I handcuffed him, and I
26 called the local sheriff's office.

27   Q.   Why did you call the sheriff's office?

28   A.   I needed somebody to take the defendant to jail.

29   Q.   Did someone from the sheriff's office show up?

30   A.   She sure did.

31   Q.   She?

32   A.   Deputy Millie Duncan.

33   Q.   What did she do?

34   A.   She put the defendant in the sheriff's vehicle and drove away.

35   MS. MATHER: That is all I have for now, Judge Foss.

36   CROSS EXAMINATION

37   MS. KRAMER: How are you today, Warden?

38   A.   I am doing fine, Ms. Kramer. Thanks for asking.

39   Q.   I wonder about a couple of details about what you said a moment
40 ago. It sounds like Deputy Duncan got to the scene pretty quickly. It

1   sounds like you have worked with the sheriff's deputies before, doesn't it?

2   A.   That's because I have.

3   Q.   So you have a pretty close relationship with the sheriff's depart-
4   ment, don't you?

5   A.   Well, I guess you would say so.

6   Q.   Why don't you tell us about that relationship?

7   A.   Whenever we run into criminal conduct outside our jurisdiction,
8   you know, not fish and wildlife violations, but other criminal activity, we
9   are supposed to call in the sheriff.

10   Q.   You are allowed to make arrests under state law, aren't you?

11   A.   Yes. But we are not equipped to put people in jail.

12   Q.   That makes sense. Beyond that though, wardens have additional
13   instructions about cooperating with local law enforcement, don't they?

14   A.   Well, I am not quite sure what you have in mind.

15   Q.   You or wardens generally get instructions on looking for drug
16   activity when you or they are in rural areas, don't you?

17   A.   Generally?

18   MS. MATHER: Your Honor, the question is too general. Warden Mola
19   can't understand the question.

20   THE COURT: Ms. Kramer, can you try to rephrase the question?

21   MS. KRAMER: Of course. So you have been told by some sheriffs, for
22   example, right here in Brainerd County what to look for to spot drug
23   activity out in the woods, haven't you?

24   A.   Yes, I have been told.

25   Q.   What have you been told?

26   A.   We had some lessons, looked at some pictures, to help us identify
27   marijuana plants and to figure out signs of meth labs. The chemicals they
28   use in meth labs smell a lot like battery acid, like sulfuric acid.

29   Q.   Any other training on how to identify drug activity?

30   A.   Well, we have periodic training, usually provided by the State
31   Police down in McGeorge City.

32   Q.   Again, what kind of training?

33   A.   Same thing; films, slide shows, discussions, all focusing on tell-
34   tale signs of drug activity.

35   Q.   I bet the State Police are happy to have your cooperation, aren't
36   they? I mean given how tight their budgets are and how much territory
37   you cover?

38   A.   I guess so.

39   Q.   And, of course, I bet they like the ability of game wardens to
40   search without probable cause, don't they?

41   MS. MATHER: Objection. The question calls for nothing but specula-
42   tion into intent and that is irrelevant.

1   THE COURT: Ms. Mather, I think that you are right. But let me hear
2   from Ms. Kramer.

3   MS. KRAMER: Your Honor, I am not trying to argue pretext
4   searches. The Supreme Court told us that is off limits. But other cases,
5   like *Burger* v. *New York* and *Indianapolis* v. *Edmond* tell us that the pur-
6   pose of a program is relevant.

7   THE COURT: Okay. I am going to allow the question and ignore it if
8   it is irrelevant.

9   MS. KRAMER: So, the State Police like having wardens involved in
10   helping locate drug dealers, don't they?

11   A.   I really don't know.

12   Q.   Well, why do you think that the State Police provides training in
13   identifying drug activity?

14   A.   To keep us safe. We have to be careful when we get in the back-
15   woods where some of the drug cartels are growing marijuana. Meth labs
16   are dangerous too.

17   Q.   And so you don't think that their training is to get you working
18   in tandem with the police?

19   A.   Like I said, I don't really know.

20   Q.   How often do you locate drug activity?

21   A.   Not too often.

22   Q.   Well, let's try to put a number on it, Warden. As everyone here
23   knows, all of us have been involved in other cases, where you found drug
24   evidence on some of my clients. Seems like it happens pretty often. So
25   why don't you give me an estimate so that we don't have to go and dig up
26   court records, okay?

27   A.   (Nodding).

28   Q.   So, about how many?

29   MS. MATHER: Your Honor, could Ms. Kramer try to put a time frame
30   around her question?

31   THE COURT: Yes, Ms. Kramer. Are you asking in his fifteen years as
32   a warden? I won't allow such an open-ended question. Or do you have
33   something more definite in mind?

34   MS. KRAMER: Okay, Mr. Mola, what about in the last year, how
35   many times have you found evidence of drugs when you have been on
36   duty as a fish and game warden?

37   A.   Maybe ten, a dozen.

38   Q.   And I assume that is typical of each year, say, in the last three
39   years, isn't it?

40   A.   I guess so. There are a lot of druggies in the woods.

41   Q.   Now back to the beginning, Mr. Mola. Exactly what did you see
42   when you saw my client leaving the trail?

43   A.   I saw him dragging an awfully heavy ice chest, and from my past
44   experience, I concluded that he had caught too many fish.

1   Q.   What apart from the fact that he was dragging the ice chest?

2   A.   That is pretty much it. It looked heavy.

3   Q.   Well, that is the ice chest over there next to Ms. Mather, isn't it?

4   A.   Looks like it.

5   Q.   By looking at the ice chest, can you tell right now, just looking,
6   how much it weighs?

7   MS. MATHER: I object. I don't see where this is going, Your Honor.

8   THE COURT: Ms. Kramer?

9   MS. KRAMER: Your Honor, I imagine that Ms. Mather will argue
10   alternatively that the warden had probable cause to arrest even if you
11   hold that the officer needed probable cause to search.

12   THE COURT: Okay. Ask away.

13   MS. KRAMER: Warden, you were going to tell me whether you can
14   tell the weight of that ice chest.

15   A.   Just by looking, I guess not. But if I see somebody dragging it, I
16   know that.

17   Q.   Well, how much do you think my client weighs?

18   A.   I don't know. Maybe he weighs 150. But he is real wiry.

19   Q.   So from what I remember you testifying to earlier, you based
20   your conclusion that Mr. Pike had too much fish in his cooler solely on the
21   weight of the ice chest, right?

22   A.   I guess so.

23   MS. KRAMER: Nothing further, Your Honor.

24   THE COURT: Ms. Mather, do you have any redirect or maybe we can
25   end a little early today. I have a busy docket this afternoon.

26   MS. MATHER: I guess in light of your schedule, I can end here.
27   Thank you.

28   THE COURT: Good and thank you. So I see a few issues here. I
29   thought that this case would turn on the special needs argument. But I
30   see other issues floating around here. Like Ms. Kramer said, Ms. Mather,
31   you may be arguing probable cause anyway. So I would like some briefing
32   on the issues, and then we will get back in court when I have open court
33   time in October. I look forward to hearing from both of you.

CHAPTER SEVEN

MIRANDA v. ARIZONA AND INVOLUNTARY CONFESSIONS

I. INTRODUCTION

The simulation exercise in this chapter gives you an opportunity to explore the rules governing confessions. It entails three main questions: the first is when the defendant was in custody, the threshold for when she should have received her *Miranda* warnings? If she was in custody before she received *Miranda* warnings, is the second statement inadmissible even though it followed a proper set of *Miranda* warnings? Even apart from the *Miranda* issues, was the defendant's statement involuntary?

This chapter consists of a brief overview of the law governing the issues described above, a discussion of the role of counsel in this exercise, the defendant's motion to suppress evidence, a short memorandum in support of that motion, and a transcript of a hearing on the defendant's motion to suppress her statements.

II. OVERVIEW OF THE LAW

A. Custody

Between 1936 and 1966, the Court decided over thirty cases in which defendants claimed that their confessions were involuntary. Many of the cases arose in the South, often involving minority defendants, who at times were subjected to brutal police conduct and who faced the death penalty. In those cases, the defendants contended their confessions were the product of police compulsion or were otherwise made involuntarily. Because the Court resolved that issue based on a case-specific totality of the circumstances test, the case law provided little guidance for lower courts. *Miranda v. Arizona*, 384 U.S. 436 (1966), attempted to resolve that on-going problem.

The *Miranda* majority intended its holding to create bright lines to get the Court out of the business of repeated fact-sensitive decisions. The primary evil that *Miranda* hoped to cure was the inherent pressure that suspects faced when interrogated in the custodial setting. As a result, according to *Miranda* and its progeny, *Miranda* warnings are required when the police engage in interrogation in a custodial setting.

Despite the hope for bright lines, *Miranda* has produced a massive body of interpretative case law, seldom capable of being reduced to bright lines. The case law defining "custody" demonstrates that point.

Miranda defined the term "custody." It occurs when a person is "taken into custody or otherwise deprived of his freedom of action in any significant way." The Court has attempted to refine the term further: a person is in custody if the police have made a " 'formal arrest or restraint of movement' of the degree associated with a formal arrest." That assessment must be made by examining "all of the circumstances surrounding the interrogation."

Oregon v. Mathiason, 429 U.S. 492 (1977), demonstrates the absence of a bright line definition for custody. There, the interrogation took place at the police station. That fact did not equate to custody. Instead, the Court focused on other factors, including the fact the defendant came to the station voluntarily and was told by the investigating officer that he was not under arrest. Somewhat surprisingly, the Court also observed that after his confession, the defendant was allowed to leave the station.

Equally true, the fact that interrogation takes place outside the station house is not controlling. For example, in *Orozco v. Texas*, 394 U.S. 324 (1969), the Court found that a suspect surrounded by armed police officers was in custody even though he was in his home.

Despite uncertainty created by *Mathiason*, (its emphasis on the post-interrogation release of the suspect), the Court has indicated that the officer's subjective view concerning the person's status as a suspect is not a factor in defining "custody." Instead, the test focuses on whether, given all of the circumstances, "a reasonable person [would] have felt he or she was not at liberty to terminate the interrogation and leave." *Thompson v. Keohane*, 516 U.S. 99 (1995).

B. The Two-Stage Interrogation

During a period when the Court began narrowing *Miranda*, the Court ruled that, in effect, a *Miranda* violation has no poisonous fruit, other than the exclusion of the original statement taken without *Miranda* warnings. *Oregon v. Elstad*, 470 U.S. 298 (1985). That was so because, according to the Court's emerging view of *Miranda*, *Miranda* provided prophylactic protection against compelled statements. *Elstad* distinguished between statements that were inadmissible because they were involuntary and those that were mere *Miranda* violations.

Nationally, many police departments responded to *Elstad* by encouraging officers to ignore *Miranda*. Police organizations recommended a two-stage interrogation. The first step was to interrogate a suspect without providing *Miranda* warnings. A confession without warnings would be suppressed. But once the suspect confessed, the police were instructed to give *Miranda* warnings and then "lead[] the suspect to cover the same ground a second time." The legality of the two-stage interrogation was at issue in *Missouri v. Seibert*, 542 U.S. 600 (2004).

While the Court found Seibert's confession inadmissible, the Court did not produce a majority opinion in *Seibert*. Justice Breyer's concurring opinion indicated one of the analytical problems with the case: the second statement looks like the fruit of the earlier statement (after all, as the defendant argued in *Elstad*, once he confessed, the "cat was out of the bag.") While Justice Breyer would have overruled *Elstad*, he joined Justice Souter's plurality opinion. Justice Souter argued the procedure used in *Seibert* rendered the *Miranda* warnings ineffective. Further, Justice Kennedy's concurring opinion provided the fifth vote: he found highly relevant that the police deliberately violated *Miranda*.

Finding a rule that has the support of a majority of the justices has been challenging for lower courts. One lower court found *Seibert* requires three steps: the first requires the court to determine if law enforcement deliberately used the two-step procedure to avoid *Miranda*. Only if the court finds the police acted deliberately should the court go further. The second step requires the court to focus on the factors found determinative by the plurality (e.g., timing and setting of the two interrogations; continuity of police personnel, etc.) Finally, the court should ask whether the police took curative measures; for example, did the police tell the suspect that the original statement was inadmissible?

C. Voluntariness

Prior to the incorporation of the Fifth Amendment, the Court found the Due Process Clause of the Fourteenth Amendment prevents the use of involuntary statements. Even after the incorporation of the Fifth Amendment, the Court has effectively made the test under the Fifth and Fourteenth Amendments the same: in light of the totality of the circumstances, was the defendant's statement voluntary? The test focuses on both the characteristics of the defendant and the details of the interrogation.

Beginning with *Brown v. Mississippi,* 297 U.S. 278 (1936)(involving a defendant admittedly beaten by a sheriff's deputy), the Court decided involuntariness claims repeatedly over a thirty year period. The rationale supporting the rule has not always been clear. Further, the test has never yielded bright line rules. As indicated above, in *Miranda*, the Court hoped to get out of the business of reviewing fact-sensitive cases. For many reasons, *Miranda* failed to solve the problem of coerced confessions.

For a period of time, defense attorneys who brought *Miranda* challenges often ignored Due Process involuntariness claims. As the Court narrowed *Miranda*, Due Process challenges have become increasingly important. Those challenges can arise in a number of settings. For example, a defendant may claim that a *Miranda* waiver was involuntary. Or he may contend that, while he waived his *Miranda* rights, the post-waiver police conduct was coercive, rendering the statement involuntary.

Cases that were seldom included in Criminal Procedure cases books during the 1970s and 1980s have made a comeback. Of course, those cases still do not create bright lines. Instead, the lower court must examine a number of factors, among them, the existence of physical force, psychological pressure, threats and promises, and deception. Although the use of physical force comes closest to a *per se* rule, the Court has held in a case where the police admittedly slapped the defendant that the statement was nonetheless voluntary. *Lisenba v. California,* 314 U.S. 219 (1941). There, considerable time elapsed between the physical force and the confession. In effect, the Court held that the earlier physical abuse did not cause the confession. Further, while some lower courts have developed bright line rules governing police deception, the Court tolerates some amount of deception. Even in one of the Court's most defendant friendly involuntariness cases, police deception was only one of many factors that the Court relied on in finding the defendant's confession involuntary. *Spano v. New York,* 360 U.S. 315 (1959).

III.   PEOPLE v. JENNIFER MANN

On September 26, YR–01, the police received a 911 call. Responding to the call, McGeorge City Police Detective Raymond Sergio found the decedent's body lying face down at the bottom of a cliff. His investigation led him to the top of the cliff where he saw distinctive footprints, indicating that someone, probably a woman, pushed the decedent off the cliff.

Shortly thereafter, the Detective went to the decedent's home where he met the defendant, the decedent's wife. He began to suspect her involvement in the crime almost immediately. Initially, they travelled to the morgue so she could identify her husband's body. A couple of days later, the Detective asked her to come to the station to talk about the case.

Over the course of several hours, the Detective discussed the case with the defendant. He did not give the defendant *Miranda* warnings. During the course of the discussions, he checked out some of her statements, many of which were false. Eventually, he confronted her with a report that, he claimed, showed that her shoes matched prints found at the murder scene. Their conversation continued for a period of time, but she later confessed her involvement in the crime.

Thereafter, the Detective read the defendant her *Miranda* rights. She repeated her earlier confession. Subsequently, the State of Pacific indicted the defendant for first degree murder, defined as "any willful, deliberate and premeditated killing of another."

What follows is the defendant's motion to suppress evidence, a brief memorandum supporting her motion, and the transcript of the evidentiary hearing in *People v. Mann.*

Your professor will assign a student or students to represent the People and a student or students to serve as defense counsel. Because the court has heard the evidence but not yet made findings of fact, you may argue the facts and, of course, should argue the application of those facts to the law. Without a live witness, you cannot argue credibility based on demeanor. But you can argue whether the witness's testimony is credible in light of internal inconsistencies and logic.

More important than factual arguments are the relevant legal arguments. Depending on instructions from your professor, you may argue all of the legal issues raised above. In this simulation, both sides have plausible arguments on each of the three distinct legal issues.

In the
SUPERIOR COURT
FOR THE COUNTY OF McGEORGE

State of Pacific
Plaintiff

Criminal Action No. 00–1269JD

vs.

Judge: Dennis Caplan

Defendant Jennifer Mann

I. Defendant's Motion to Suppress

Defendant, being a person aggrieved by unlawful interrogation, moves to suppress for use as evidence all statements obtained as a result of said illegal interrogation on the following grounds:

1. On September 30, YR–01, the Defendant was arrested by officers of the McGeorge City Police Department.

2. The Defendant was interrogated by members of the McGeorge City Police Department.

3. The police did not provide the Defendant with *Miranda* warnings despite the fact she was in custody for a prolonged period of time.

4. After securing one confession without proper warnings, members of the McGeorge City gave her *Miranda* warnings, fully aware she would confess again.

5. The police conduct deliberately circumvented *Miranda* and made the *Miranda* warnings ineffective.

6. The police interrogation took place over a period of hours. Further, members of the McGeorge Police City Department relied on trickery, lies, and deception to coerce the defendant into confessing.

7. For the above reasons and otherwise, the Defendant's inculpatory statements were taken in violation of her Fifth and Fourteenth Amendment rights under the United States Constitution.

Dated: November 20, YR–01

Respectfully submitted,

Rand Cooper

Rand Cooper
Attorney-at-Law
53 Joplin Rd.
McGeorge City, Pacific 95817
Telephone: (797) 555–5253
Attorney for Defendant

In the
SUPERIOR COURT
FOR THE COUNTY OF McGEORGE

State of Pacific
Plaintiff

Criminal Action No. 00–1269JD

vs.

Judge: Dennis Caplan

Jennifer Mann
Defendant

Memorandum of Points and Authorities on Behalf of Defendant

I. Introduction

JENNIFER MAN was indicted for First Degree Murder for the death of her husband that took place on September 26, YR–01.

II. Facts

On September 26, YR–01, police received a 911 call from someone who located a dead body in Rockledge Park, McGeorge City. In response, Detective Raymond Sergio found the body, determined it was the body of Jeff Mann, the Defendant's husband. On September 30, YR–01, Detective Sergio engaged in protracted interrogation of the Defendant without giving her *Miranda* warnings. After hours of interrogation and after presenting her with a false report claiming her shoe prints were found at the murder scene, the Defendant admitted involvement in the decedent's death. Thereafter, Detective Sergio read Defendant her *Miranda* warnings. She did not invoke those rights. Instead, she repeated her confession.

III. Argument

More than 40 years ago, the United States Supreme Court held that whenever a suspect was subjected to custodial interrogation, the police must warn her of her right to remain silent and her right to have an attorney present during the interrogation. *Miranda v. Arizona,* 384 U.S. 436 (1966). Failure to warn a suspect leads to the suppression of any statement taken in violation of *Miranda's* clear procedures. Failure to give the Defendant her *Miranda* rights in the instant case should result in suppression of her initial inculpatory statement.

Further, having secured one statement by deliberately ignoring the Defendant's *Miranda* rights, the police took advantage of her initial statement to secure a second statement after the Detective gave the Defendant her *Miranda* warnings. In light of all of the facts, the police rendered ineffective those warnings. As a result, the second inculpatory statement should be suppressed.

Finally, judged by all of the surrounding circumstances, the police conduct was so coercive that it rendered the Defendant's statement involuntary. As a result, both of the Defendant's statements should be suppressed.

IV. Conclusion

For the foregoing reasons, the Defendant requests the court to suppress all of the evidence obtained as a result of the violation of the Defendant's Fifth and Fourteenth Amendment rights.

Respectfully submitted,

Rand Cooper

Rand Cooper

Attorney-at-Law
53 Joplin Rd.
McGeorge City, Pacific 95817
Telephone: (797) 555–5253
Attorney for Defendant Jennifer Mann

1 Transcript of the hearing on Defendant Jennifer Mann's Motion
2 to Suppress

3 Wednesday, January 6, YR–00

4 The matter of the People of the State of Pacific v. Jennifer Mann,
5 Defendant, case number 00–1269JD, came before the Honorable Dennis
6 Caplan, Judge of the Superior Court of Pacific, County of McGeorge.

7 THE COURT: Good morning, ladies and gentlemen. Okay. For the
8 record, this is People of the State of Pacific v. Jennifer Mann. Enter your
9 appearances for the record.

10 Ms. CONNELL: Your honor, Sarah Connell for the People.

11 Mr. COOPER: Rand Cooper for Ms. Mann.

12 THE COURT: Mr. Cooper, this is your motion to suppress?

13 Mr. COOPER: It is, but I also have a motion in limine concerning
14 admissibility of Ms. Mann's prior record and an outstanding discovery
15 request.

16 THE COURT: Well, I see Ms. Connell's witness in the courtroom, or
17 I assume that the officer is your witness.

18 Ms. CONNELL: It is, Your Honor. Mr. Cooper and I discussed the
19 discovery issue earlier. Perhaps we can speed things along by putting the
20 discovery matter before you now, then having the hearing on Mr. Cooper's
21 motion, and finish up with the motion in limine later?

22 THE COURT: Mr. Cooper, does that work for you?

23 Mr. COOPER: It does, Your Honor. I am still waiting for some evi-
24 dence concerning DNA evidence; Ms. Connell promised me that informa-
25 tion earlier.

26 Ms. CONNELL: I did promise him the information, but the lab has
27 suffered budget cuts recently and the staff is behind. In light of that, we
28 agreed to ask you to extend our discovery schedule by three weeks.

29 THE COURT: We are still a long way from trial, but I hope that will
30 not force changes in the trial date for this case. Obviously, a murder case
31 presents special challenges, but you know the importance to everyone
32 concerned to stay on schedule. But in light of your agreement, yes, I will
33 extend the deadline. Did either of you prepare a written order for me to
34 sign for the record?

35 Ms. CONNELL: We did. We left it with your clerk.

36 THE COURT: Thank you. I will see to it later then. So let's get back
37 to the issues for the day. The motion in limine was about what?

38 Mr. COOPER: I believe that Ms. Connell proposes to use a prior con-
39 viction. Ms. Mann pled guilty over fifteen years ago to battery. It involved
40 a domestic dispute with a former husband. She pled guilty to avoid trial
41 and the risk of jail time. It was a long time ago.

42 THE COURT: Before we get into the details, I can see that the mat-
43 ter will not take just five minutes. Let's get on to the hearing. The motion
44 in limine may be premature. I will need to know more facts about the
45 crime charged. So let's move on now.

1   Detective Raymond Sergio was called as a witness, being duly sworn,
2 was examined and testified as follows:

3   DIRECT EXAMINATION

4   Ms. CONNELL: Detective, would you please state your name for the
5 court and spell your name for the court reporter?

6   A. Raymond Sergio, S–E–R–G–I–O.

7   Q. You currently serve as a detective with the McGeorge City Police
8 Department, is that correct?

9   A. Yes.

10   Q. How long have you held that position?

11   A. For five years.

12   Q. And how long have you been with the McGeorge City Police
13 Department; I mean, I assume that you were not hired as a detective?

14   A. Oh, that is correct. It was in YR–12, and I became a detective
15 after seven years on the force.

16   Q. Now, if I may draw your attention to September 26, YR–01, were
17 you assigned to investigate a homicide involving a person found deceased
18 in Rockledge Park?

19   Mr. COOPER: Objection.

20   THE COURT: Mr. Cooper, I have no idea what you are objecting to.

21   Mr. COOPER: The Detective seems to have decided that he was
22 investigating a homicide long before he knew how the decedent died.

23   THE COURT: Okay. I would sustain the objection if we were in front
24 of a jury, but we are not. We all know that this turned into a murder
25 investigation pretty quickly and that your client has been charged with
26 that murder. I don't want to discourage you from making objections, Mr.
27 Cooper. But try to use some judgment.

28   Mr. COOPER: I will try to do so, Your Honor.

29   Ms. CONNELL: May I continue, Your Honor?

30   THE COURT: Of course. Or Detective, do you need the court reporter
31 to read back the last question?

32   A. No, I remember the question. Ms. Connell wanted to know
33 whether I was assigned to an investigation in Rockledge Park. I sure was.
34 That is why I am here today.

35   Ms. CONNELL: Would you describe in your own words what you dis-
36 covered when you arrived at the scene?

37   A. Well, I don't know if you are familiar with the park. But it is
38 pretty rustic even though it is still in city limits. It has some pretty steep
39 rock faces that are very popular with rock climbers. Some of those faces
40 are sheer and are several hundred feet straight up. A couple of climbers
41 apparently called 9–1–1 when they found a body at the bottom of one of
42 the rock faces.

43   Q. What was the condition of the body when you arrived at the
44 scene?

1   A.   Well, the deceased was face down. The deceased was obviously a
2   man. It looked like he fell from a couple of hundred feet above and landed
3   pretty hard.

4   Q.   Did you examine the body further?

5   A.   I did, along with a member of the medical team. The medic
6   turned the deceased over onto his back. His face had been pretty badly
7   damaged when he hit the ground. His nose was smashed in; his neck was
8   broken.

9   Mr. COOPER: Objection. Detective Sergio has not been qualified as a
10   medical expert.

11   THE COURT: Ms. Connell, do you intend to qualify him?

12   Ms. CONNELL: Your Honor, I can, but I did not think that Mr. Coo-
13   per really contests the cause of death. I think that he concedes that Jeff
14   Mann died of a broken neck from a fall from about 250 feet above. My
15   understanding is that his defense is that the decedent slipped and that
16   was simply an accident.

17   THE COURT: Mr. Cooper, is that the case?

18   Mr. COOPER: May I withdraw the objection?

19   THE COURT: This could be a long day, Mr. Cooper.

20   Ms. CONNELL: If I may continue ...

21   (The Court nodded).

22   Ms. CONNELL: Detective, so you were describing the deceased and
23   you concluded that he had broken his neck in a fall from the cliffs. Is that
24   correct?

25   A.   Yes, that's right.

26   Q.   Was there anything else that you learned from looking at the
27   body?

28   A.   Rigor had set in. From several bodies that I have examined in
29   the past, I could tell that he must have fallen the night before, maybe as
30   much as ten hours earlier. I was looking at him in the early morning; I
31   would say that he must have been dead for eight, ten, hours.

32   THE COURT: Just to be sure, I guess that the coroner's office even-
33   tually confirmed that information?

34   Ms. CONNELL: Are you asking the Detective or me?

35   THE COURT: I know that Mr. Cooper did not object, but I want to be
36   clear. Is the time of death going to be an issue today?

37   Mr. COOPER: No, Your Honor.

38   Ms. CONNELL: Detective, back to you. When did you learn the dece-
39   dent's name? Well, let me check—did you learn the decedent's name?

40   A.   I did. I put on plastic gloves and reached into Mr. Mann's pocket
41   where I saw what looked like a wallet. It was, and I opened it and found
42   his driver's license.

43   Q.   Did you do anything else at the scene on that date?

1   A.   Yes, I did.

2   Q.   What did you do?

3   A.   Well, I left the medical team members with the body, and I found
4 a path up to the top of rock face so that I could have a look around.

5   Q.   What did you see there?

6   A.   Well, you know how wet it was last fall? I found the spot where
7 Mr. Mann must have slipped.

8   Q.   Why did you conclude that was the spot?

9   A.   It was directly above where we found the body. I could see the
10 body from where I was standing at the top of the rock face. And when I
11 looked at the ground, I could see footprints.

12   Q.   Did you compare those prints to the shoes that Mr. Mann was
13 wearing?

14   A.   Oh, I should have mentioned that before. When I was looking at
15 the body, right before I went up the path, I looked at his shoes because I
16 wanted to see if I could find any shoe prints. He was wearing distinctive
17 work boots with a Strong Man label on the bottom of the shoe.

18   Q.   Take us back to the top of the rock face. You saw Mr. Mann's shoe
19 prints, you said?

20   A.   I did, and I could see the Strong Man label in the mud pretty
21 clearly. I took a couple of photos of those prints.

22   Q.   But looking at his prints led you to suspect foul play, didn't it?

23   A.   It did.

24   Q.   Because?

25   A.   While there were a couple of clear prints, I saw more than one
26 set of prints. One pair was much smaller than Mann's shoes. And it
27 looked like the two people might have walked up to the edge of the cliff ...

28   Mr. COOPER: Objection, Your Honor. This is speculation.

29   THE COURT: Mr. Cooper, how is this relevant to your motion to sup-
30 press? You are objecting to statements made later, aren't you? Are you
31 suggesting some kind of illegal search?

32   Mr. COOPER: No, Your Honor. But the People contend that this was
33 not an accident and the Detective is engaging in pure speculation.

34   THE COURT: Save that objection for trial, counsel.

35   Ms. CONNELL: With permission, Your Honor, I want to ask the
36 Detective what he saw, what inferences he drew from the footprints at the
37 top of the cliff?

38   THE COURT: Of course, Ms. Connell, that is perfectly appropriate.

39   Ms. CONNELL: Detective, if you need the question read back, I am
40 sure that our court reporter can do so.

41   A.   No. I was just telling you that I could tell that two people were
42 at the spot where Mr. Mann must have fallen. The person who wore the
43 smaller shoes, well, I could tell from the prints that he, or probably judg-

1   ing from the size, she slipped after coming up behind the decedent.

2   Q. Based on your observations, what did you conclude?

3   A. I concluded that this was a homicide, not an accident. And I
4   stated that in my report.

5   Q. Did you notice if any of the smaller shoe prints would allow
6   identification?

7   A. I was not sure at the time, but I learned later ... I see Mr. Coo-
8   per about to jump out of his seat, should I continue?

9   Q. Well, until he objects, yes.

10   THE COURT: Mr. Cooper seems to have kept his seat.

11   Ms. CONNELL: Detective, you were saying?

12   A. One of the other investigators did make a mold of one of the
13   shoes. We got a good match, but it was a common woman's shoe.

14   Q. Did you learn anything else at the time?

15   A. Not at the scene.

16   Q. What did you do next in this case?

17   Mr. COOPER: Objection, the question is too indefinite.

18   THE COURT: Sustained.

19   Ms. CONNELL: Subsequently, did your investigation focus on the
20   defendant, Jennifer Mann?

21   A. Yes, it did.

22   Q. Why did that happen?

23   A. When I got back to the station house, someone had done a quick
24   check and learned that the decedent was married. And we had his
25   address from his license. I took it on myself to go to their house to tell her
26   about her husband's death.

27   Q. How did that go?

28   A. When I got there, it was late in day, early evening, maybe around
29   7:00 P.M. And Mr. Mann must have been dead close to 24 hours, maybe a
30   little less.

31   Q. Was the defendant there when you arrived at her house?

32   A. She was.

33   Q. Did she answer the door right away?

34   A. It seemed like a couple of minutes.

35   Q. How did she act when she did open the door?

36   A. She did not show much surprise.

37   Mr. COOPER: Objection, pure speculation.

38   THE COURT: Overruled.

39   Ms. CONNELL: Detective, you were saying?

40   A. I identified myself. She did not look surprised, as I said. I told
41   her that her husband's body was found that morning.

1   Q. How did she respond?

2   A. She said, "When he didn't come home last night, I feared some-
3   thing was wrong."

4   Q. Did she show remorse?

5   A. No.

6   Q. Did you notice anything else about the defendant?

7   A. I did. I looked at her feet. They were small, about the size of the
8   shoe prints that I saw at the scene.

9   Q. Did she make any other statements at that time?

10   A. Well, she asked about his body, and we discussed the next step.
11   I told her that she should come down to the morgue the next day to iden-
12   tify her husband's body.

13   Q. Did she do that?

14   A. She asked if she could drive herself to the morgue or if she had
15   to go with me.

16   Q. And what did you tell her?

17   A. I told her that she was free to drive herself and that I would meet
18   her there. And that is what she did.

19   Q. Did you go to the morgue as well?

20   A. I did.

21   Q. Did she identify the body?

22   A. She did.

23   Q. Did she show any emotion?

24   A. Again, no. She looked at the body; she said something about the
25   blood and his face getting bruised pretty bad.

26   Q. Did she make any other statements at the morgue?

27   A. No.

28   Q. Was that the end of your conversations with the defendant?

29   A. No.

30   Q. Would you tell us when you next spoke to the defendant?

31   A. Two days, so three days after we found the body. I wanted to do
32   some investigation before I met with her again.

33   Q. So how did you happen to talk to her two days later?

34   A. As we were leaving the morgue, I told her that I needed to talk
35   to her.

36   Q. She asked me why.

37   A. I told her that it was part of routine investigation.

38   Q. She asked if she was under suspicion.

39   A. What did you say?

40   Q. I said that she was not.

1   A.   And did you tell her where the interview was to take place?

2   Q.   I don't remember if I suggested that she come down to the sta-
3   tion or if she offered.

4   A.   Did you take notes, uh, I mean if you look at your notes, can you
5   clarify who suggested the station as the place for the meeting?

6   Q.   No. I did not make a note on that point.

7   A.   What is your normal procedure?

8   Mr. COOPER: Objection. The Detective testified that he can't remem-
9   ber what he did at the time.

10   THE COURT: Sustained.

11   Ms. CONNELL: Okay. Detective, so the defendant and you met at the
12   station two days after the trip to the morgue, correct?

13   A.   Yes.

14   Q.   Did you, well, back up. Tell me in your own words what hap-
15   pened when she arrived at the station.

16   A.   The duty officer called me to the front desk where the defendant
17   was waiting. I asked her to come back to one of the interview rooms,
18   Room 5. On the way back to the room, things were cordial; I asked her
19   how she was doing. She said that she was doing okay.

20   Q.   Did you tell her that she was under arrest? Did you handcuff her
21   at any point?

22   A.   No, I did not tell her that she was under arrest, and I did not
23   handcuff her, not then.

24   Q.   So she went to the interview room, correct?

25   A.   Yes.

26   Q.   Did you give her *Miranda* warnings then?

27   A.   No.

28   Q.   Why not?

29   A.   I did not tell her that she was under arrest.

30   Q.   Did you ask her questions about her husband's death?

31   A.   I did.

32   Q.   Detective, would you tell us about the conversation with the
33   defendant?

34   A.   Sure. First, I asked her about her husband, what kind of guy he
35   was, whether he drank, whether he had any enemies, whether he had a
36   temper, stuff like that.

37   Q.   What did she tell you?

38   A.   Well, she portrayed him as a good guy, no enemies, drank a little
39   but not much, no trouble with the law.

40   Q.   Did you believe her?

41   Mr. COOPER: Objection. Relevance.

1   THE COURT: I'll allow it. At some point, Mr. Cooper, you are going
2 to argue that the defendant was under arrest and you will probably argue
3 that the Detective's beliefs were relevant.

4   Mr. COOPER: Thank you, Your Honor.

5   Ms. CONNELL: I withdraw the question. Did you continue to ques-
6 tion her?

7   A.   I did. I asked her about her relationship with her husband, how
8 long they had been married, whether they had any difficulties in their
9 marriage.

10   Q.   Her answers?

11   A.   Again, she acted as if everything just fine.

12   Q.   Did you know any facts to suggest that she was not telling the
13 truth?

14   A.   Sure.

15   Q.   Detective, well? Want to tell us what you knew?

16   A.   Okay. So before I started the interview, I did some homework.
17 Our records indicated that the defendant had gotten a protective order a
18 few years earlier, when the defendant was separated from the decedent.
19 That was after a couple of complaints of domestic violence that she had
20 brought.

21   Q.   Did you learn any other facts?

22   A.   Yes. Officer Johnny Luongo ran down a couple of leads. The dece-
23 dent was a heavy drinker and had a reputation as a ladies' man, often
24 throwing money around.

25   Q.   Was the protective order still in force?

26   A.   No. I gather that the Manns had made up; they were living
27 together again.

28   Q.   Did you ever suggest that you suspected the defendant of push-
29 ing her husband?

30   A.   Eventually, yes, I did.

31   Q.   Well, that did not happen right away, did it?

32   A.   No.

33   Q.   Well, pick up with your testimony about your discussions with
34 the defendant.

35   A.   Okay. So I asked her a lot of background questions about her and
36 her husband. I asked her about the night that he died.

37   Q.   What did she say?

38   A.   She said that he left around 8:00 or 9:00; she said he told her
39 that he was meeting friends for a drink.

40   Q.   Did she identify the friends?

41   A.   Yes.

42   Q.   Did you ever learn whether he met them?

1   A. Yes.

2   Q. When?

3   A. During the defendant's time at the station, I would leave occa-
4 sionally, offer her coffee, get coffee, let her take a bathroom break, and
5 then while I was not with her, I asked Luongo to check out her story.

6   Q. And?

7   A. She was lying every time. For example, Luongo got hold of the
8 decedent's best buddy, and he said that Mr. Mann never showed up that
9 night.

10   Q. Were you the only police officer who was in the interview room?

11   A. For most of the time, yes.

12   Q. When you say, most of the time, did there come a time when
13 another officer conducted the interview or came into the interview room
14 with you?

15   A. Yes.

16   Q. Who, when, and what happened?

17   A. Detective Ray Burke was watching the interrogation from the
18 command room; the interview rooms are equipped with cameras. And
19 officers watch from outside the room. So eventually Burke joined me.

20   Q. And what happened?

21   A. A couple of things. He took over questioning the defendant for a
22 while. He is a pretty nice guy and sometimes folks talk to him if they
23 won't talk to me.

24   Q. Did the defendant talk to Burke?

25   A. Not right away. Well, she did talk to him. But she did not say
26 anything very revealing for awhile.

27   Q. But she did eventually?

28   A. Yes.

29   THE COURT: Detective, it is almost time for a break. I have some
30 business to conduct. To speed things up, would you give us a narrative of
31 what happened?

32   A. Oh, sure.

33   Ms. CONNELL: So pick up the narrative.

34   A. Okay. I don't remember how long it took, but Burke and I were
35 getting pretty tired. I know that I was at least. And the defendant seemed
36 like she was not going to give us anything. So earlier, I noticed that the
37 defendant had on tennis shoes and so I asked her early on whether I could
38 take them.

39   Q. Did she let you take the shoes?

40   A. She did.

41   Q. And?

42   A. They were the same size as the prints that I saw on the cliff. So
43 later, I left the room again. When I came back, I showed her a piece of

1   paper and told her that I had sent her shoes out to be tested. I told her
2   that the report showed signs of mud that matched the spot where her
3   husband was pushed off the cliff and that the shoe tread matched prints
4   that we found there.

5   Q. Did the defendant say anything at that point?

6   A. Not right away.

7   Q. Did she eventually?

8   A. Yes. We had been at this for awhile, and she said that she was
9   hungry and asked if we could take a dinner break.

10   Q. Did you?

11   A. Yes.

12   Q. And then, what happened?

13   A. We called out for a pizza and let her eat while we took a break.

14   Q. How long a break did you take?

15   A. It must have been forty-five minutes or so.

16   Q. What happened when you returned to the interview room?

17   A. I told her that I had been checking on some of her facts and that
18   she had not been telling the truth.

19   Q. What specifically did you tell her?

20   A. For one, I told her that her husband did not go out with his bud-
21   dies that night. For another, I told her that I knew all about her com-
22   plaints about her husband. I told her that she wasn't being square with
23   us. I told her that I knew that her husband was violent and that from
24   what we had heard, he might have had it coming to him. I told her that
25   I heard that she had heard that he was cheating on her.

26   Q. How did she respond?

27   A. She looked down for a long time and then she said, with no emo-
28   tion, "you got me."

29   Q. "You got me," meaning what?

30   A. I had the same question, so I asked her, "You mean that you
31   killed your husband?"

32   Q. And what did she say?

33   A. She said yes. She said, it was like you and your partner sug-
34   gested.

35   Q. Was that the end of the interview?

36   A. Yes and no.

37   Q. Detective, what does that mean?

38   A. We took another break. She looked like hell and told us that she
39   was going to faint. We brought the defendant some coffee and a pack of
40   cigarettes, and we let her walk around a little on her own.

41   Q. Was anyone watching her while she walked around?

42   A. No.

1   Q. Could she have walked out of the jail?

2   A. Sure.

3   Q. How much time elapsed between, well, how long was this break?

4   A. It was probably an hour or so. When she came back to the inter-
5 view room after walking along the hall, she seemed to fall asleep for a few
6 minutes.

7   Q. So you gave her coffee and let her refresh herself and let her
8 sleep, and after that, did you resume discussions with her?

9   A. Yes. I read her the *Miranda* warnings from the standard
10 *Miranda* card that we use.

11   Q. Which states what precisely?

12   A. It states, 1. You have the right to remain silent. 2. Anything you
13 say can and will be used against you in a court of law. 3. You have the
14 right to talk to a lawyer and have him present with you while you are
15 being questioned. 4. If you cannot afford to hire a lawyer, one will be
16 appointed to represent you before any questioning. 5. You can decide at
17 any time to exercise these rights and not make any statements or answer
18 any questions.

19   Q. Did the defendant respond to the warnings?

20   A. She did respond. She said, "I know my rights; I will talk to you
21 now."

22   Q. Before that, did she tell you that she understood her rights?

23   A. Oh, yeah. I, yes, she did. After I read the warnings, I asked her
24 if she understood them. She said yes and then she said she would talk.

25   Q. At which point, what did she say?

26   A. She said, "He had it coming. He was a no-good abusive SOB."

27   Q. Did she indicate anything else?

28   A. We got her to start at the beginning. We told her that we knew
29 that she had been planning this for some time, and she admitted as much.

30   A. So she stated?

31   Q. She explained that she got him to agree to go up on the bluffs to
32 have a picnic for dinner and she gave him a lot to drink. Then she sug-
33 gested that they walk along the bluffs.

34   A. At which point, she pushed him?

35   Q. Yes. She said that he was in front of her and she shoved him
36 hard. He went over but that she did not see him go over because she
37 slipped and fell on her behind. Like I described earlier, that is consistent
38 with the shoe prints that I saw.

39   Ms. CONNELL: Nothing further, Your Honor. I tender the witness.

40   THE COURT: Mr. Cooper, before you begin, I have to take a break. I
41 have a matter that I need to take care of in chambers. Everyone here
42 needs a break as well, I am sure. We will reconvene in 30 minutes.

43   (Court is in recess).

1   THE BAILIFF: All rise. The Honorable Judge Dennis Caplan, Supe-
2   rior Court of the State of Pacific.

3   THE COURT: Be seated and, Mr. Cooper, you are up to bat.

4   CROSS EXAMINATION

5   Mr. COOPER: Good morning, Detective.

6   A.   Good morning, Mr. Cooper.

7   Q.   Let's go back to something that you told us earlier today. You
8   went to the defendant's house and pretty quickly you focused on her as a
9   suspect, didn't you?

10 Ms. CONNELL: Objection, Your Honor. Relevance.

11 THE COURT: Ms. Connell, as I recall, you asked the Detective a very
12 similar question. Overruled.

13 Q.   Detective, your answer to my question, unless you need the court
14 reporter to read it back to you?

15 A.   No, I got it.

16 Q.   The answer?

17 A.   I got suspicious early on. She showed no feelings, no remorse.

18 Q.   When you asked her to come to the station house, you did not
19 have any other information, other than your suspicions, did you?

20 A.   That is not true. She, her foot size was the same as whoever
21 pushed the decedent off the cliff.

22 Q.   That is it, then?

23 A.   A spouse is almost always a suspect in a murder case, and I got
24 it right this time.

25 Q.   That does not show that you had probable cause at the time, does
26 it?

27 Ms. CONNELL: Objection, argumentative.

28 THE COURT: Sustained. Mr. Cooper, I thought that you were object-
29 ing to the taking of the statement, not to the Fourth Amendment issues?

30 Mr. COOPER: Well, Your Honor, the statement might have been the
31 product of an illegal arrest.

32 THE COURT: Oh. I am not going to comment on that idea at this
33 point. Pick up where you left off. Detective, no, wait. I just sustained the
34 objection. Mr. Cooper, back to you.

35 Mr. COOPER: So let's go down to the station. When Mrs. Mann got
36 there, you had focused on her as the suspect, hadn't you?

37 A.   I guess so.

38 Q.   You took her right into an interrogation room, didn't you?

39 A.   An interview room.

40 Q.   Oh, so you have different rooms for suspects and people you are
41 just interviewing?

1   A.   No.

2   Q.   So this was an interrogation room, wasn't it?

3   Ms. CONNELL: Objection, asked and answered and argumentative.

4   THE COURT: I am going to sustain that objection. But Detective, let
5   me jump in here. I can see that you and Mr. Cooper could start sparring,
6   and I don't want us to waste time. What procedure do you have in place
7   when you interview witnesses, like crime victims?

8   A.   Victims of crimes, well, often we interview them at their homes
9   or in the hospital.

10   THE COURT: What about witnesses who come to the station?

11   A.   That depends on whether we have room to interview them.

12   THE COURT: When I was in the D.A.'s office, that is not what the
13 procedure was, as I recall. The policy was to interview them in more com-
14 fortable surroundings.

15   A.   Like I said, it depends.

16   THE COURT: Mr. Cooper, sorry for the interruption. You may take
17 over.

18   Mr. COOPER: Thank you, Your Honor. Detective, you said, as I recall,
19 that you did not tell the defendant that she was under arrest. But you did
20 not testify that you did not tell her that she was free to go, did you?

21   A.   Huh?

22   THE COURT: He is trying to ask if you told the defendant that she
23 was free to go.

24   A.   I don't remember.

25   Mr. COOPER: You testified about having the defendant in the inter-
26 rogation room for a long period of time, didn't you?

27   A.   I did.

28   Q.   Your records indicate how long the interrogation went on, don't
29 they?

30   A.   Interview, not interrogation.

31   Q.   That will be for the court to decide. Answer the question.

32   Ms. CONNELL: Objection.

33   THE COURT: Overruled. Mr. Cooper, let me direct the witness to
34 answer; don't argue with him. Detective, how long did the interview take
35 place?

36   A.   From start to finish?

37   THE COURT: Detective, from start to when she confessed the first
38 time and then from that point to when you got the second statement.
39 Walk us through the whole thing. What time did the defendant show up
40 at the station and go from there.

41   A.   Okay. So she showed up at 9:30 AM.

42   Mr. COOPER: Your Honor, I would like to resume my cross-
43 examination.

1   THE COURT: Of course. I am sorry. I was trying to be helpful.

2   Mr. COOPER: No doubt, and you were. Detective, so you began your
3 conversation with the defendant at 9:30 or thereabout. When did you ask
4 her for her shoes?

5   A.   Not long after that, maybe at 10:00 AM.

6   Q.   In your earlier testimony, you said that you and Burke were get-
7 ting pretty tired, didn't you?

8   A.   We all get tired at some point.

9   Q.   But during your discussions with the defendant, before you
10 showed her the phony report about her shoes?

11   A.   Yes, I did.

12   Q.   So it must have been awhile after you began your shift that
13 morning?

14   A.   I guess so.

15   Q.   Do you recall how long it was?

16   A.   It was a little before noon.

17   Q.   Okay, so you came back later to show her a copy of the report, oh,
18 let me ask you first. You made up the report, didn't you?

19   A.   Not the form.

20   Q.   But the contents on the form indicating that the shoe prints
21 matched?

22   A.   Yes.

23   Q.   As I recall, you said that it took about 45 minutes between show-
24 ing her the report and when she made her first statement about "You got
25 me," didn't you?

26   A.   No, it was longer than 45 minutes. We gave her food and a break
27 to relax for 45 minutes after showing her the report. Then we came back
28 and it was awhile before she confessed. I told her a lot of other stuff—I
29 told her that we had checked out her story and that she was not square
30 with us. So, maybe it was a couple of hours between the report and the
31 confession.

32   Q.   And I am correct that at no point up to this first confession did
33 you read the defendant her *Miranda* warnings?

34   A.   That is correct.

35   Q.   Any reason why not?

36   A.   She was there of her own free will.

37   Q.   You didn't attend any of the police training sponsored by the
38 Police Law Institute that told police about two-stage interrogation, did
39 you?

40   A.   No.

41   Q.   Let me rephrase the question. Did you ever attend any kind of
42 training session where you heard about two-stage interrogation?

1   A.   Uh, you mean like a conference?

2   Q.   Or part of your training here at the McGeorge City Police
3 Department?

4   A.   Oh. Yes.

5   Q.   Yes, what?

6   A.   Our department had a training session where we heard about it.

7   Q.   So that was not what you were doing when you had the defen-
8 dant in the station house for several hours before you gave her *Miranda*
9 warnings?

10   A.   No.

11   Q.   Oh, I can't remember if you ever fully answered the Judge's ear-
12 lier question. How long from 9:30 to the time when the defendant first
13 confessed?

14   A.   I, can I check my notes?

15   THE COURT: Yes.

16   A.   About seven hours; my notes suggested that it was around 4:00
17 PM by the time she confessed.

18   Q.   You testified that not long after she confessed the first time, you
19 gave the defendant *Miranda* warnings, didn't you?

20   Ms. CONNELL: Objection. He did not testify that it was not long.

21   Mr. COOPER: Your Honor, may we have a side bar?

22   THE COURT: Yes.

23   (The following took place in chambers).

24   Mr. COOPER: Ms. Connell is trying to signal the Detective. Under
25 the case law, the second statement without *Miranda* warnings is inadmis-
26 sible if it came quickly upon the first confession.

27   Ms. CONNELL: I resent the suggestion that I was acting inappropri-
28 ately.

29   THE COURT: It has been a long day. I get Mr. Cooper's point. But,
30 Ms. Connell, don't be overly sensitive. I will handle this in open court.

31   (In open court)

32   THE COURT: We are back in session. Detective, to get the ball roll-
33 ing again, Mr. Cooper asked you a question. I am going to ask Ms. Rhei-
34 ngold to read it back to you.

35   (Reading: Q. "You testified that not long after she confessed the first
36 time, you gave the defendant *Miranda* warnings, didn't you?")

37   A.   I don't think that is what I said. We took a break; she even fell
38 asleep; we got her coffee. So it was awhile.

39   Mr. COOPER: If you need more help, I will ask Ms. Rheingold to read
40 back your testimony, but I recall you saying that it was about an hour
41 between her first confession and the reading of the *Miranda* warnings.

42   A.   No, that wasn't counting the time when she was asleep.

1 Q. And so, as I recall, you said that she slept briefly, didn't you?

2 A. Not so brief.

3 Q. Again, if you need help, Ms. Rheingold can read back your
4 answers. Did you or did you not say under oath earlier today that the
5 defendant fell asleep for a few minutes?

6 A. I could have, but a few minutes is open to interpretation.

7 Mr. COOPER: Your Honor, would you ask Ms. Rheingold to read back
8 the Detective's testimony?

9 THE COURT: Yes. Ms. Rheingold, you will be a rich woman after
10 printing this transcript for the attorneys. Would you read back the Detec-
11 tive's testimony, specifically dealing with the lapse between the first con-
12 fession and the *Miranda* warnings?

13 (Reading: "A. We took another break. She looked like hell and told us
14 that she was going to faint. We brought the defendant some coffee and a
15 pack of cigarettes and we let her walk around a little on her own.

16 (Q. Was anyone watching her while she walked around?

17 (A. No.

18 (Q. Could she have walked out of the jail?

19 (A. Sure.

20 (Q. How much time elapsed between, well, how long was this break?

21 (A. It was probably an hour or so. When she came back to the inter-
22 view room after walking along the hall, she seemed to fall asleep for a few
23 minutes.

24 (Q. So you gave her coffee and let her refresh herself and let her
25 sleep, and after that, did you resume discussions with her?

26 (A. Yes. I read her the *Miranda* warnings from the standard
27 *Miranda* card that we use.)

28 THE COURT: Thank you, Ms. Rheingold. Mr. Cooper, continue if you
29 have more questions.

30 Mr. COOPER: So, Detective, was your testimony accurate earlier
31 today?

32 A. Sure.

33 Q. Thank you for your candor. I have a couple more questions for
34 the Detective. You indicated earlier that early in the day, you expressed a
35 lot of sympathy for the defendant while you were interviewing her, before
36 you gave her *Miranda* warnings, didn't you?

37 A. I guess so.

38 Q. Did you? I can ask Ms. Rheingold for another, uh, to read back
39 your testimony.

40 A. No need to. Yes, sure. From what I heard, the decedent was not
41 the greatest guy in the world.

42 Q. But could one characterize your questioning as a play on her
43 sympathies, showing her that you were sympathetic to her?

1   A. You lawyers can characterize almost anything however you want.
2 That is your game.

3   THE COURT: Detective, try not arguing with counsel.

4   A. Sorry, Judge.

5   Mr. COOPER: Don't the standard books on getting defendants to con-
6 fess emphasize making a show of sympathy?

7   A. I guess so. But you know, I am usually talking to defendants
8 who, like her (pointing at the defendant) can kill somebody without bat-
9 ting an eye and express no remorse.

10   Q. I get your point. I guess you feel like a little trickery is fair with
11 somebody that cold-blooded?

12   A. Maybe.

13   Mr. COOPER: Nothing more for now, Your Honor.

14   THE COURT: Ms. Connell, any re-direct?

15   Ms. CONNELL: A few questions, thank you, Your Honor.

16   REDIRECT EXAMINATION

17   Q. You were not intentionally trying to violate *Miranda* when you
18 …

19   Mr. COOPER: Objection, leading.

20   THE COURT: Sustained.

21   Ms. CONNELL: Were you trying to violate *Miranda* when you inter-
22 viewed the defendant without giving her *Miranda* warnings initially?

23   A. Of course not. No, I thought that the law allows us to interview
24 someone who is not in custody, without giving *Miranda* warnings.

25   Q. And the total time between the first and second confessions, if
26 you can pinpoint that for us?

27   A. Okay. May I check my notes?

28   THE COURT: Mr. Cooper, any objection?

29   Mr. COOPER: No, Your Honor.

30   Ms. CONNELL: Does that help refresh your recollection, Detective?

31   A. Yes.

32   Q. Your answer?

33   A. Probably 90 minutes. And that is a conservative estimate. It
34 could have been longer.

35   Q. Going back to when the defendant arrived at the station, did you
36 in any way indicate that she was not free to go?

37   A. No.

38   Q. Did you make any statements or any gestures suggesting that
39 she was in custody?

40   A. No.

41   Q. Nothing further, Your Honor.

1   RECROSS EXAMINATION

2   Mr. COOPER: Detective, you testified that you were aware of the
3 two-stage interrogation technique, didn't you?

4   A. Yes, I was or am.

5   Q. And given that you had a training session on the technique, you
6 have tried using it in the past, haven't you?

7   A. Not in this case.

8   Q. Kindly answer the question.

9   A. Kindly? Yeah.

10   Q. Back to when Mrs. Mann first came into the station, you just
11 testified that you did not say or do anything suggesting that she was in
12 custody, correct?

13   A. Sure.

14   Q. But you earlier testified that you had developed plenty of evi-
15 dence that she committed murder, didn't you? You developed that evi-
16 dence before she arrived?

17   A. I, sure.

18   Q. So you thought that you had a murderer on your hands, a cold-
19 blooded killer, whom a few minutes ago you indicated that you thought of
20 as fair game?

21   A. I guess so.

22   Q. Your testimony, not mine. Yes or no?

23   Ms. CONNELL: Mr. Cooper is badgering the witness.

24   Mr. COOPER: I am not. This is cross examination, and the witness is
25 being evasive.

26   THE COURT: Please answer directly, Detective. We don't want to
27 keep going back through the transcript for your prior testimony.

28   A. Okay.

29   Mr. COOPER: Detective, you did your homework before you brought
30 or invited the defendant to the station, didn't you?

31   A. I did my work. I am a professional.

32   Q. So you had developed a good bit of evidence pointing towards
33 homicide and towards my client, correct?

34   A. Yes.

35   Q. So, when Mrs. Mann was in the station house, and you'd done
36 your homework and had evidence that she was a killer—your testimony,
37 Detective—you would not have let a murderer leave the station and go
38 back out on the street, would you?

39   A. If I did not have enough evidence to hold her, I would have to.

40   Q. But you had developed that evidence, hadn't you?

41   A. Maybe.

42   Q. Maybe? I thought that you had done your homework?

1   A.   I want more than just probable cause before we make such seri-
2 ous charges. So I would have let her go if I did not get enough evidence to
3 move forward.

4   Q.   So you had to be sure you got a confession so you could hold
5 someone you suspected of being a cold-blooded killer, correct?

6   A.   Maybe.

7   Q.   I would like to cover one more area, Detective. You mentioned
8 that the defendant didn't show emotion when you told her about her hus-
9 band, correct?

10   A.   That's because she didn't.

11   Q.   You assumed that she didn't show emotion because she killed her
12 husband, again, isn't that correct?

13   A.   Sure.

14   Q.   You don't think that the defendant is very smart, do you?

15   A.   Smart enough. If we hadn't found footprints, she might have got-
16 ten away with murder.

17   Q.   So you thought that she was smart?

18   A.   Like I said, smart enough.

19   Q.   Really? You were able to get her first confession by using a phony
20 report, correct?

21   A.   I don't know exactly why she confessed. I showed her the report
22 awhile before she confessed.

23   Q.   But you showed her the report to get her to confess, didn't you?

24   A.   Sure.

25   Q.   Now, you testified that it was, what, a short time between taking
26 her shoes and bringing in the report. It was maybe an hour or so. You told
27 her that in the interim you had tests performed on her shoe, correct?

28   A.   Yes.

29   Q.   You would have thought that a person of ordinary intelligence
30 would know that you could not get test results in such a short period of
31 time, wouldn't you?

32   A.   Maybe. But a lot of smart people don't know much about foren-
33 sics.

34   Q.   Would you be surprised if I told you that the defendant's IQ is
35 only about 85?

36   A.   I wouldn't be surprised if a lawyer told me that the moon was
37 made of blue cheese.

38   THE COURT: Detective, answer the question without being flip.

39   A.   My apologies, Judge.

40   Mr. COOPER: Your answer to my question is what?

41   A.   I would be surprised. She seemed a lot smarter than that when
42 I was talking to her.

1   Mr. COOPER: Uh, Detective, so, let me withdraw that.

2   THE COURT: Mr. Cooper, are you almost done? We are past lunch
3   time and it would be nice to give folks some rest.

4   Mr. COOPER: I am done, Your Honor, except for one stipulation. Ms.
5   Connell and I discussed this earlier. I can bring in a witness if necessary,
6   but Ms. Connell has agreed to allow into evidence a report indicating that
7   Ms. Mann's IQ is 85.

8   THE COURT: Ms. Connell?

9   Ms. CONNELL: I have no objections.

10   THE COURT: Thanks. So it is now 12:45. We will break until 2:00.
11   Then, Mr. Cooper, you and Ms. Connell want to discuss an additional
12   motion?

13   Mr. COOPER: We do.

14   THE COURT: Okay, so 2:00. And oral argument on the motion to
15   suppress, can you be ready this afternoon as well?

16   Ms. CONNELL: I am set to go.

17   Mr. COOPER: I will be ready as well.

18   (Court is in recess)

CHAPTER EIGHT

TAKING STATEMENTS FROM A SUSPECT: *MASSIAH* AND *MIRANDA*

I. INTRODUCTION

The simulation exercise in this chapter gives you an opportunity to explore the rules governing the police's ability to take statements from an unsuspecting defendant. It also allows you to develop the facts in a hearing on the Defendant's motion to suppress her statements. Since the 1930's, the Court has regulated coercive interrogation practices. But what other techniques can the police use to get incriminating statements from a suspect?

This exercise consists of an overview of the law, the defendant's motion to suppress, and some legal documents that the prosecution has provided the defendant. Your professor will assign students different roles, including three witnesses who will appear on behalf of the State, counsel for the prosecution and the defense, and the defendant. Your professor will provide the witnesses with role summaries.

II. OVERVIEW OF THE LAW

Most casebooks include a discussion of the road to *Miranda*, starting with the Court's early Due Process cases. In cases like *Lisenba v. California,* 314 U.S. 219 (1941), *Spano v. New York,* 360 U.S. 315 (1959), and *Townsend v. Sain,* 372 U.S. 293 (1963), the Court had to determine on a case-by-case basis whether a defendant's confession was involuntary, and therefore, inadmissible. Because the case law provided little guidance to the police and to lower courts, the Warren Court seemed intent on finding a solution to the problem of police overreaching in such cases.

One solution endorsed by four justices concurring in *Spano* was to extend the right to counsel to the interrogation stage of a criminal proceeding. In 1964, the Court adopted that approach in *Massiah v. United States,* 377 U.S. 201 (1964). There, the government had indicted the defendant for violating federal drug laws. Using a cooperating co-defendant, government agents recorded the defendant's incriminating statements. The Court held that the government violated the defendant's Sixth Amendment right to counsel. While Massiah had already been indicted, the Court seemed to extend the Sixth Amendment right to counsel to the interrogation setting even without commencement of formal proceedings in *Escobedo v. Illinois,* 378 U.S. 478 (1964).

With hindsight, we know that *Escobedo* was a tentative step on the road to *Miranda.* Decided two years later, *Miranda v. Arizona,* 384 U.S. 436 (1966), held that a defendant's Fifth Amendment right to be free from compelled testimony extended to the stationhouse. Counsel in that setting, according to the Court, was necessary to protect the defendant's Fifth Amendment right to be free from compelled testimony.

Between 1966 and 1977, litigants and the Court largely ignored *Massiah.* *Escobedo* could be explained away as an uncertain step towards *Miranda.* Designed to get the Court out of the business of deciding fact-sensitive involuntariness cases, *Miranda* has produced an extraordinary amount of litigation. When Richard Nixon ran for President on a law-and-order platform in 1968, Americans had in mind the *Miranda* decision as an example of activist justices gone awry. President Nixon's four appointments to the Court began to cabin *Miranda* almost immediately. Indeed by 1977, some commentators speculated that the Court would overrule *Miranda.*

Almost certainly, the Court granted certiorari in *Brewer v. Williams,* 430 U.S. 387 (1977), with an eye towards overruling *Miranda.* Instead, the Court found that the police violated the defendant's Sixth Amendment right to counsel when the police detective deliberately elicited Williams' confession. Authored by Justice Stewart, a *Miranda* dissenter but the author of *Massiah,* the *Williams* opinion relied on *Massiah* as controlling authority. Importantly, in *Williams,* while not indicted, the defendant had been formally charged.

Post-*Williams,* whether a defendant has a Fifth Amendment *Miranda* right to counsel or a Sixth Amendment right to counsel when the police attempt to get a confession has become increasingly important. As demonstrated in *Perkins v. Illinois,* 496 U.S. 292 (1990), the *Miranda* right to counsel attaches only when the police engage in custodial interrogation. There, the police placed an undercover operative in Perkins' jail cell with an eye towards getting him to confess to a murder. Had the defendant's Sixth Amendment right to counsel attached, the police conduct would have been illegal under *Massiah.* But because formal proceedings had yet to commence, the defendant could not make that argument.

In a related line of cases, the Court has also held that the police may investigate a defendant, for example, by using an undercover operative, even when the defendant is already indicted as long as the police are investigating an uncharged crime. In such a case, any evidence obtained is inadmissible in the prosecution for the original offense, but is admissible in the trial on the new charges. As stated in *McNeil v. Wisconsin,* 501 U.S. 171 (1991), the Sixth Amendment right to counsel is offense-specific.

As the Court held in *Massiah,* once formal proceedings have commenced, the police may not deliberately elicit incriminating statements from the defendant without a waiver of the right to counsel. The Court's test begs another question: what does "deliberate elicitation" mean? Here, the Court has created some uncertainty despite language in *Williams* suggesting that the police must act "with the specific intent to evoke an incriminatory statement."

In *United States v. Henry*, 447 U.S. 264 (1980), federal agents relied on an informant who was housed in a local jail with Henry. One of the agents told the informant "to be alert to any statements made by [Henry], but not to initiate any conversation with or question Henry regarding the bank robbery." At trial the informant testified that he engaged the defendant in conversation about the robbery. In light of the agent's instructions, one would have thought that the government did not deliberately elicit the confession. The Court found a violation of the defendant's Sixth Amendment right to counsel because the agents intentionally created a situation likely to induce Henry to make incriminating statements.

Did *Henry* expand the *Massiah* test? *Kuhlmann v. Wilson*, 477 U.S. 436 (1986) creates uncertainty about the Court's application of its test. There, the police placed an informant in Wilson's cell and told the informant to "keep his ears open," but to avoid asking the defendant questions. At one point, the defendant told the informant a story about his involvement in the crime under investigation. The informant indicated his disbelief. Thereafter, following a visit from family members, the defendant confessed to the informant. Perhaps important to the Court's finding, the trial court found that the informant followed the police's instructions not to question the defendant. The Court upheld the use of the confession and found that the informant was merely a passive listener.

Lining up the two cases is difficult, in part, because the *Wilson* Court made no effort do to so. Viewed objectively, the cases seem similar in important ways: the government agents in both cases cautioned the informants not to initiate the conversation; despite that, the informants engaged in conversation and the defendants confessed. Perhaps the Court could line the cases up by emphasizing some particular facts of the two cases. In *Henry*, for example, the government paid the informant only if he reported incriminating information. Thus, the federal agents were intentionally creating a situation designed to lead to a confession. Perhaps the trial court's findings in *Wilson* were critical: unlike the informant in *Henry*, the informant in *Wilson* was passive.

Lower courts have faced a variety of questions left unanswered by the Court. For example, they have had to determine when private citizens become agents of the state for purposes of *Massiah*. Some courts set the bar for agency quite high. A recent Georgia Supreme Court opinion canvassed the approach of many lower courts and concluded that *Massiah* requires a finding of agency between the government and the informant and observed that "... to qualify as a government agent, the informant must at least have some sort of agreement with, or act under instructions from, a government official ..." *Higuera-Hernandz v. State*, 2011 WL 2671401 (Ga.). *See also People v. Watson*, 2011 WL 2858163 (Cal. App. 4 Dist.) (unpublished). In reading *Massiah, Henry,* and *Wilson,* consider whether the Court adopted such a narrow interpretation of deliberate elicitation.

As you can see, the Court has developed different standards to determine whether a defendant's *Miranda* right to counsel or her Sixth Amendment right to counsel has been violated. Beyond that, the Court's fruit-of-the-poisonous-tree case law treats the two rights differently as well. The Court held that a mere *Miranda* violation does not lead to the suppression of evidence that resulted from the violation, other than the initial un-Mirandized statement. *Oregon v. Elstad,* 470 U.S. 298 (1985). Not entirely clear is whether a *Massiah* violation leads to a full analysis under the Court's fruit-of-the poisonous-tree case law. Compare *Williams* (assuming that it does) with *Fellers v. United States,* 540 U.S. 519 (2004) (remanding the case for a determination whether *Elstad* applies to *Massiah* violations). On remand, the court of appeals found that *Elstad* did apply. *United States v. Fellers,* 397 F.3d 1090 (8th Cir. 2005). Also relevant may be the Court's decision in *Kansas v. Ventris,* 556 U.S. 586 (2009), where the Court held that the State did not violate the defendant's Sixth Amendment right to counsel by using a statement taken in violation of *Massiah* when the State used the statement to impeach the defendant.

The following simulation exercise allows you to explore several of the issues discussed above.

III. PEOPLE v. TARA LOUISE STEVENS

In the
SUPERIOR COURT
FOR THE COUNTY OF McGEORGE

State of Pacific
Plaintiff

Criminal Action No. 00–2690JD

vs.

Judge: Joseph Myers

Defendant Tara Louise Stevens

I.   Defendant's Motion to Suppress

Defendant, being a person aggrieved by unlawful efforts by the police to secure her confession, moves to suppress for the use as evidence all confessions obtained by said conduct and all other evidence obtained as a result thereof on the following grounds:

1.   On July 15, YR–01, the Defendant was arrested by McGeorge City police for possession of cocaine with intent to distribute.[1]

2.   Thereafter, on July 18, YR–01, without providing the Defendant with counsel, detectives of the McGeorge City Police Department contacted the Defendant's sister and brought her to the jail where the Defendant was housed.

3.   With the cooperation of the police, the Defendant's sister was able to secure the Defendant's statements implicating her in a significant drug transaction.

4.   Further, on July 23, YR–01, in reliance on those statements, the McGeorge City Police Department intercepted a shipment of cocaine, addressed to the Defendant, coming from Colombia and shipped via Federal Express.

5.   On August 10, YR–01, the prosecution sought and received a superseding indictment charging the Defendant with two counts of possession of cocaine with intent to distribute. Count 1 is based on the evidence seized on July 15, YR–01; Count 2 is based on the evidence seized July 23, YR–01.

6.   For the above reasons and otherwise, the Defendant's inculpatory statements were taken in violation of her Fifth, Sixth and Fourteenth Amend-

---

1. According to § 111351 of the Pacific Health & Safety Code, "every person who possesses any Schedule II controlled substance with intent to distribute shall be punished by imprisonment in the state prison for three, six or nine years." Cocaine is a Schedule II drug. The State proves the intent to distribute by showing that the defendant possessed an amount in excess of what one would have for personal use.

According to § 111350 of the Pacific Health & Safety Code, "every person who possesses any Schedule II controlled substance shall be punished by imprisonment in the county jail for not more than one year or in state prison."

ment rights under the United States Constitution. Further, the physical evidence seized by the police was the product of that illegality.

7. As a result, the Defendant urges this court to suppress all of the Defendant's inculpatory statements and the physical evidence seized as a product of that illegality.

Dated: August 26, YR–01

Respectfully submitted,

Rand Cooper

Rand Cooper
Attorney-at-Law
53 Joplin Rd.
McGeorge City, Pacific 95817
Telephone: (797) 555–5253
Attorney for Defendant

In the
SUPERIOR COURT
FOR THE COUNTY OF McGEORGE

State of Pacific
Plaintiff

00–2690JD

vs.

Judge: Joseph Myers

Defendant Tara Louise Stevens

Memorandum of Points and Authorities on Behalf of Defendant

I. Introduction

Tara Louise Stevens has been charged with the unlawful possession of cocaine with intent to distribute and possession of cocaine under §§ 111350–111351 of the Pacific Health & Safety Code.

II. Facts

On July 15, YR–01, pursuant to an arrest warrant, drug agents of the McGeorge City Police arrested the Defendant on suspicion of possession of cocaine. Over the next several days, while the Defendant was detained in the McGeorge City jail, detectives of the McGeorge City encouraged the Defendant's sister Karen Stevens Perry to visit her sister and to elicit incriminating statements from the Defendant without the protection of counsel.

During those visits, the Defendant admitted her involvement in efforts to import two kilograms of cocaine from Colombia. Further in reliance on that information, agents of the McGeorge City Police Department intercepted a shipment of cocaine that arrived at the McGeorge City Federal Express office.

Thereafter, the Defendant was indicted on two counts of possession of cocaine with intent to distribute.

III. Argument

The Defendant had a right to counsel to protect her from making incriminatory statements. The Fifth, Sixth and Fourteenth Amendments to the Constitution gave the Defendant the right to counsel. Agents of the McGeorge City Police Department acted deliberately in creating a situation likely to lead to the Defendant making incriminatory statements without the guiding hand of counsel. Further, once the Defendant made her statements, agents of the McGeorge City Police Department used those illegally obtained statements to seize physical evidence implicating the Defendant.

IV.   Conclusion

For the foregoing reasons, the Defendant requests the court to suppress all of the evidence obtained as a result of the violation of her Fifth, Sixth and Fourteenth Amendment rights.

Respectfully submitted,

Rand Cooper

Rand Cooper

Attorney-at-Law
53 Joplin Rd.
McGeorge City, Pacific 95817
Telephone: (797) 555–5253

IV. THE INCIDENT REPORT

> Incident and Investigation Report: Case Number 00–2690JD, Report Date: July 28, YR–01

> Notes/Narrative

Based on the arrest of an unnamed informant who has provided information leading to successful arrests and prosecutions in the past (case citations available), Detective Courtney Duncan swore out a warrant of arrest for Tara Louise Stevens. That warrant stated the probable cause that said defendant was involved in drug trafficking, specifically, that she had on a date certain sold said unnamed informant $200 worth of powdered cocaine.

On July 15, YR–01, agents of this office arrested the defendant. Thereafter, she was housed in the City Jail. Detective Courtney Duncan interviewed her on that date, read her Miranda warnings, but the Defendant insisted that she did not want to talk to the police.

On a number of occasions, her sister, Karen Stevens Perry visited her sister at the jail. Said sister approached officers on July 20, YR–01 and asked if they were interested in what her sister had told her. She then revealed that her sister admitted her involvement in the sale of cocaine and she was expecting a shipment of cocaine from Colombia. The defendant had requested her sister to get word to the Defendant's husband who would pick up the package for her.

Based on the information, Detective Duncan swore out search warrant #YR–01–126. In cooperation with agents for the McGeorge office of Federal Express, Detective Duncan intercepted a package addressed to the defendant. Upon opening said package, Detective Duncan found 2 kilograms of cocaine.

End of Report

V. THE ARREST WARRANT

STATE OF PACIFIC—COUNTY OF McGEORGE
v.
Tara Louise Stevens

ARREST WARRANT AND AFFIDAVIT

<u>Courtney Duncan</u>   swears under oath that the facts
(Name of Affiant)
expressed by him/her in this Arrest Warrant and Affidavit and in the attached and incorporated statement of probable cause are true and that based thereon he/she has probable cause to believe and does believe that the person described has committed a felony in violation of the laws of the State of Pacific.

Wherefore, affiant requests that this Arrest Warrant be issued.

Courtney Duncan ,
(Signature of Affiant)

(ARREST WARRANT)

THE PEOPLE OF THE STATE OF PACIFIC TO ANY PEACE OFFICER IN THE COUNTY OF McGEORGE:

proof by affidavit. having been made before me by <u>Courtney Duncan</u>
(Name of Affiant)

that there is probable cause to believe that the Person described herein committed a felony in violation of the laws of the State of Pacific.

YOU ARE THEREFORE COMMANDED TO ARREST:

Tara Louise Stevens

This Arrest Warrant and incorporated
Affidavit was sworn to as true and
subscribed before me this <u>30</u> day of
<u>June</u> , YR–01, <u>10:30</u> **A.M.** Wherefore, I find probable cause for the issuance of this Arrest Warrant and do issue it.

James Fisher ,
(Signature of Magistrate)

Judge of the Superior Court, City and County of McGeorge, <u>James Fisher</u>

(AFFIDAVIT)

(Statement of Probable Cause)

Your affiant Courtney Duncan, Detective, McGeorge City Police Department, is empowered to conduct investigations under the laws of the State of Pacific. Your affiant is currently assigned the Drug Enforcement Task Force within the McGeorge City Police Department.

The probable cause set forth in this affidavit is based on my personal participation in this investigation. Based on my familiarity with the facts and circumstances of this case, I allege the facts outlined in the following paragraphs to show there is probable cause to believe that the defendant has committed violations pertaining to §§ 111350–111351 of the Pacific Health & Safety Code (possession of cocaine and possession of cocaine with intent to distribute).

Background of investigation

Your affiant led an investigation of cocaine and other drug activity in the City of McGeorge, beginning in June, YR–01. Your affiant instructed agents to make controlled drug buys from street dealers in the area of Olive Drive and 5th Street, McGeorge City, an area known for high crime and drug dealing.

On June 26, YR–01, Agent Lynn Simmons made a controlled drug purchase from a known drug user. Faced with arrest and prosecution, said drug user offered to trade information about his source of drugs. On June 27, YR–01, Agent Simmons told me about said drug purchaser's willingness to cooperate. On that date, your affiant interviewed said purchaser. He stated he had made several purchases directly from Tara Louise Stevens. Your affiant also asked said purchaser if he had ever cooperated with local or other local law enforcement. He said that he had done so on a number of occasions.

Based on the information provided by said purchaser, your affiant contacted three other agents in the McGeorge City Police Department and learned that said purchaser was confidential informant CI–18. Further, your affiant investigated arrests and convictions resulting from information provided by CI–18 and learned that on five occasions, he provided reliable information leading to arrest and conviction of sellers of cocaine and other illegal narcotics in and around McGeorge City. Specifically, he gave information in cases YR–03 1267, YR–03 3478, YR–02 2356, YR–02 3467, and YR–01 236.

Your affiant swears that the above facts and circumstances are true and correct to the best of my knowledge, information and belief and I ask that a warrant be granted which authorizes the arrest of Tara Louise Stevens.

Signed: _Courtney Duncan_

    COURTNEY DUNCAN

Sworn to and subscribed before me
date ___30___ day of June, YR–01.

James Fisher
Judge, Superior Court, City and County of McGeorge

Return
This warrant was received on (*date*)   June 30, YR–01,   and the person was arrested on (*date*)   July 15, YR–01 .
Date: July 16, YR–01   _Lynn Simmons_   Arresting officer's signature   Lynn Simmons, Badge 456

CHAPTER NINE

LINEUPS, ONE–ON–ONE SHOW–UPS AND PHOTO ARRAYS

I. INTRODUCTION

The simulation exercise in this chapter gives you the opportunity to explore the rules governing lineups, one-on-one show-ups and photo arrays. It provides some background on the right to counsel at lineups and show-ups. It also allows you to explore several issues surrounding identification procedures. The simulation invites you to consider if the defendant has a right to counsel during any of the identification procedures that took place. Those procedures include a photo array and then a one-on-one show-up when police bring the defendant back to the crime scene to allow one of the victims to identify him. On the assumption that the suspect does not have a right to counsel, you should focus on whether the procedures employed by the police violated the defendant's Due Process rights. You should also explore whether a defendant is entitled to have an expert testify at trial concerning the risks inherent in eyewitness identification.

The state has charged the defendant with armed robbery based on various eye-witness identifications and an identification made during a photo array. This chapter consists of a brief overview of the law governing the issues described above, the defendant's motion to suppress evidence, a short memorandum in support of that motion, the photo array that the police showed witnesses to the crime, a transcript of a hearing on the defendant's motion to suppress the various identifications, and a second exercise concerning the admissibility of trial testimony and of the testimony of an expert witness. This simulation is designed to allow you to make an oral argument for the People or the Defendant on how the court should rule on the Defendant's motion to suppress the various identifications. In addition, it is designed to allow your professor to assign you to submit a memorandum of points and authority either supporting or opposing the motion. The final exercise allows you to take the role of counsel at a hearing to argue two legal points, one the admissibility of expert testimony and the other the admissibility of eyewitness identification at trial when the earlier identifications have been suppressed.

II. OVERVIEW OF THE LAW

Judges, researchers and commentators have argued for years that eyewitness identification is unreliable. In recent years, DNA testing has led to the exoneration of many innocent defendants. One study demonstrates the most important factor leading to improper convictions is faulty eyewitness identification. Despite its unreliability, eyewitness identification is often powerful evidence. When a prosecutor asks whether the crime victim sees his assailant in the courtroom, the jury sees the victim point a finger directly at the defendant and state in unequivocal terms, "there he is; I will never forget his face after what he did to me."

Toward the end of the Warren Court era, the Court addressed constitutional issues surrounding identification proceedings. In the early years of the Burger Court, the Court limited those cases. This simulation allows you to explore the various doctrines applicable to eyewitness identification and to photo arrays.

The leading cases in this area include *United States v. Wade,* 388 U.S. 218 (1967), and *Gilbert v. California,* 388 U.S. 263 (1967). Wade had been formally charged and was already represented by counsel when an FBI agent put Wade in a lineup. At trial, the government asked witnesses to identify the defendant as the perpetrator of an armed robbery but did not seek to introduce testimony about their identification of the defendant at the lineup. In *Gilbert,* the State did introduce that evidence. In neither case did the defendant have counsel present at the lineup.

The Court found the government violated the defendants' constitutional rights. Not entirely clear at the time was the constitutional right implicated. The Court referred to the lineup as a critical stage, suggesting the right was the Sixth Amendment right to counsel. But it also stated the presence of counsel might assure meaningful confrontation at trial, suggesting the right was grounded in the Confrontation Clause. Subsequently, the Court held the right was the Sixth Amendment right to counsel. The effect was to narrow the scope of the right.

Both Wade and Gilbert had been formally charged. That left open whether the right to have counsel present at a lineup applied to pre-indictment line-ups. Had *Wade* and *Gilbert* been grounded in the right to confront witnesses, the right to counsel should have extended to pre-indictment lineups. The Burger Court resolved that issue in *Kirby v. Illinois,* 406 U.S. 682 (1972). The plurality held that, in effect, *Wade* was a "pure" right to counsel case. As you have probably already learned, the pure right to counsel is triggered by some formal step by the state demonstrating a defendant is now "faced with the prosecutorial forces of organized society, and immersed in the intricacies of substantive and procedural criminal law." The Court has subsequently adopted the plurality's view on the nature of the right involved.

The remedy for a violation of the right to counsel depends on the evidence the prosecution intends to introduce. Absent a finding of harmless error, a court must reverse a defendant's conviction if the prosecution has introduced evidence of the identification at the lineup held without counsel. But the law is more complicated if, as in *Wade,* the prosecution seeks only to introduce an in-court identification. The Court held in *Wade* that the prosecution carried a heavy burden but could prove by clear and convincing evidence that the in-court identification was free from the taint of the earlier illegal identification. According to Justice Brennan, *Wong Sun v. United States,* 371 U.S. 471 (1963), controlled. *Wade* identified several relevant factors, including the prior opportunity to observe the suspect, and the existence of discrepancies between a pre-lineup description of the suspect and the suspect's appearance, among other factors. Apart from concerns voiced by Justice White in his *Wade* dissent, lower courts frequently find an independent source for the in-court identification.

In the third case in the Court's 1967 identification trilogy, the Court indicated a second line of argument available to a defendant faced with a pre-trial identification. In *Stovall v. Denno,* 388 U.S. 293 (1967), the Court held its *Wade-Gilbert* holding did not apply retroactively. Stovall became more important after *Kirby* made clear that *Wade-Gilbert* apply only after formal proceedings have commenced. Even before the right to counsel has attached, a defendant may argue the earlier confrontation leading to the identification of the defendant, based on the totality of the circumstances, "was so unnecessarily suggestive and conducive to irreparable mistaken identification" the defendant was denied Due Process. In *Simmons v. United States,* 390 U.S. 377 (1968), the Court refined the point: the trial court must determine whether the identification procedure "was so impermissibly suggestive as to give rise to a very substantial likelihood of irreparable misidentification." Here, the burden is on the defendant to show the identification was unnecessarily suggestive. The court must then make a determination whether the procedure was impermissibly so, again, an inquiry that takes into consideration the specific circumstances of the case before the court.

One effect of the Court's totality of the circumstances test is to allow the use of "alley" confrontations or one-person show-ups. For example, the police often pick up a suspect shortly after a crime has been reported, in the area where the crime took place. Lower courts often uphold such identifications as long as the identification occurs within a relatively short period of time after the crime.

Photo arrays present many similar issues to lineups and one-on-one show-ups. Another early Burger Court case held that, no matter when the photo array takes place, a defendant does not have a right to counsel at that procedure. *United States v. Ash,* 413 U.S. 300 (1973). According to the Court, a photo array is not a trial-like confrontation involving the presence of the defendant. Somewhat surprisingly, the Court found a photo array poses "few possibilities for unfair suggestiveness."

While a defendant does not have a right to counsel when a witness identifies her at a photo array, the defendant may contend the photo array violates Due Process. As a practical matter, the defendant has a difficult burden proving the violation. Some lower courts have upheld identifications even when the police have shown a witness a single photograph. Courts uphold the use of the photo array as long as the prosecution can show the witness had a sufficient opportunity to observe the defendant. As with the *Stovall* holding, the test focuses on the totality of the circumstances. Therefore, even an improper remark by the officer showing the witness the photo array may not be sufficient to lead to suppression of the out-of-court identification. And even upon a finding that the out-of-court identification was tainted, the court may nonetheless find the witness's in-court testimony is admissible in reliance on the *Wong Sung* analysis.

The effect of the post-Warren Court rulings has been to limit the extent to which the Constitution controls pre-trial identification evidence. But because of concerns about the inherent risks of eyewitness identification, defense attorneys have pursued state law remedies as well. This simulation explores some of those remedies, including expert testimony about the risks involved in eyewitness identification or jury instructions to that effect.

III. PEOPLE v. WADE KIRBY: THE MOTION TO SUPPRESS

In the
SUPERIOR COURT
FOR THE COUNTY OF McGEORGE

State of Pacific
Plaintiff

                          Criminal Action No. 00–2359JD

vs.

                          Judge: Carl Bricker

Defendant Wade Kirby

I.   Defendant's Motion to Suppress

Defendant moves to suppress for use as evidence all eyewitness identification of the defendant:

1.   On April 6, YR–01, McGeorge City Police officers responded to a report of an armed robbery at the Osteria Tres Porcellini restaurant in downtown McGeorge City.

2.   The officers took statements from several witnesses at the scene of the robbery. Later that evening, the officers showed photographs, including a photo of Defendant Wade Kirby, to some of the witnesses. At least some of them picked out Defendant Kirby's photograph as one of the robbers.

3.   Based on that information, an officer for the McGeorge City Police Department swore out a warrant for Defendant Kirby's arrest.

4.   Twelve hours later, an officer stopped Defendant Kirby as he was walking about one-half mile from the Osteria and took him back to the restaurant to be identified by the owner of the restaurant, Anthony Alteri.

5.   While Defendant Kirby was handcuffed and detained in the back of the police car, restaurant owner Anthony Alteri identified Kirby as the alleged armed robber.

6.   Defendant Kirby objects both to the display of photographs and to the one-on-one show-up. The display of the photographs to the alleged victims was unnecessarily suggestive and Defendant Kirby urges this court to suppress evidence relating to that identification made by any witness who witnessed the photo array. Further, the one-on-one show-up of Defendant Kirby to Anthony Alteri was unnecessarily suggestive and Defendant Kirby urges this court to suppress evidence relating to that identification.

7.   Because any in-court identification that witness Alteri might make would be the fruit of the primary illegality, Defendant Kirby urges this court to prevent the prosecution from relying on that testimony.

8.   Defendant Kirby also urges this court to suppress any and all eyewitness identification made by patrons of the Osteria Tres Porcellini because

those identifications were the product of the violation of Defendant Kirby's right to counsel and Due Process right to fundamental fairness.

9.   Alternatively, if this court finds that the prosecution may introduce evidence from any of the eyewitnesses, Defendant Kirby moves in limine that he be allowed to introduce the testimony of expert Ruth Lofty, a recognized psychologist who has studied the fallibility of eyewitness identification. Defendant Kirby moves to allow her to testify that eyewitness identification is inherently suggestive and especially so based on the facts of this case.

Dated: May 23, YR–01

Respectfully submitted,

Connor Ashford

Connor Ashford
Attorney-at-Law
156 Vintage Lane
McGeorge City, Pacific 95817
Telephone: (797) 555–8176
Attorney for Defendant

In the
SUPERIOR COURT
FOR THE COUNTY OF McGEORGE

State of Pacific
Plaintiff

Criminal Action No. 00–2359JD

vs.

Judge: Carl Bricker

Wade Kirby
Defendant

Memorandum of Points and Authorities on Behalf of Defendant

I. Introduction

Wade Kirby was indicted for seven counts of armed robbery arising out of the April 6, YR–1 robbery of Osteria Tres Porcellini.

II. Facts

At 9:00 P.M., on April 6, YR–01, McGeorge City police received a 911 call from someone who stated he was the owner of a restaurant that had just been robbed. In response, the police sent several officers to the restaurant where they interviewed several patrons and the owner of the restaurant. Based on those interviews, Detective Raymond Sergio assembled a photo array that he brought to the restaurant. Under highly suggestive circumstances, the detective showed several witnesses the photos within hearing distance of one another. Not surprisingly, a number of witnesses picked out the photo of Mr. Kirby.

Based on those identifications, Detective Sergio swore out a warrant for the arrest of Mr. Kirby. At 10:00 A.M., a McGeorge City police officer arrested Mr. Kirby while he was walking near his home, more than ½ miles from the scene of the alleged robbery. The officer took him to the restaurant, and while Mr. Kirby was handcuffed in the backseat of the patrol car, Alteri identified him as the alleged robber.

III. Argument

The practices engaged in by the McGeorge City Police Department increased the likelihood of an improper identification of Mr. Kirby as the person responsible for the April 6, YR–01 robbery. The photo array and the manner in which the police showed several persons the photographs at the same time were fundamentally unfair, in violation of Mr. Kirby's Due Process rights. Further, after the issuance of an arrest warrant, Mr. Kirby should have been provided counsel at any subsequent critical stages. The one-on-one confrontation at the scene of the crime violated his right to counsel and his right to fundamental fairness guaranteed by Due Process Clause of the Fourteenth Amendment to the Constitution.

IV. Conclusion

For the foregoing reasons, Mr. Kirby requests the court to suppress all of the evidence obtained as a result of the violation of Mr. Kirby's Sixth and Fourteenth Amendment rights.

Respectfully submitted,

Connor Ashford

Connor Ashford

Attorney-at-Law
156 Vintage Lane
McGeorge City, Pacific 95817
Telephone: (797) 555–8176

IV. THE PHOTO ARRAY

V.   PEOPLE v. KIRBY: THE HEARING ON THE MOTION

Transcript of the hearing on Defendant Wade Kirby's Motion to Suppress

Wednesday, January 14, YR–00

The matter of People of the State of Pacific v. Defendant Wade Kirby, case number 00–2359JD, came before the Honorable Carl Bricker, Judge of the Superior Court of Pacific, County of McGeorge.

THE COURT: Good morning, ladies and gentlemen. Okay. For the record, this is People of the State of Pacific v. Wade Kirby. Good morning, Ms. Foster. Mr. Ashford, you have a few motions for us today? Enter your appearances for the record.

MS. FOSTER: Margaret Foster for the People of Pacific.

MR. ASHFORD: Connor Ashford for Mr. Wade Kirby, the Defendant herein.

THE COURT: I noticed in your papers that you have a motion in limine about the use of an expert witness, as well as your motion to suppress. Mr. Ashford, that motion may be premature. So I am not going to hear evidence on that matter until after I decide on your main motion.

MR. ASHFORD: Thank you, Your Honor.

THE COURT: Ms. Foster, go ahead and call your first witness.

MS. FOSTER: The People call Detective Raymond Sergio.

Detective Raymond Sergio was called as a witness, being duly sworn, was examined and testified as follows:

DIRECT EXAMINATION

MS. FOSTER: Detective, would you please state your name for the court and spell your name for the court reporter?

A.   Raymond Sergio, S–E–R–G–I–O.

Q.   You currently serve as a detective with the McGeorge City Police Department, is that correct?

A.   Yes.

Q.   How long have you held that position?

A.   For five years.

Q.   And how long have you been with the McGeorge City Police Department?

A.   Since YR–12.

Q.   Let me take you back to April 6, YR–01. Were you assigned to investigate a report of an armed robbery at the Osteria Tres Porcellini?

A.   Yes.

Q.   Can you tell us what you learned … well, let me back up a second. You did investigate the reported crime?

1   A.   Yes. I was not the first member of the department on the scene.
2   A couple of black and whites had already arrived.

3   Q.   You mean officers on patrol?

4   A.   Yes. They responded to the 911 call and had secured the scene.

5   Q.   And when you got there, what did you do?

6   A.   I should tell you that I was there with Detective Martin Falcón
7   as well. There were seven or eight people in the restaurant, or they were
8   still there. I think that some folks ran away during the robbery. But seven
9   or eight people were still there and had lost something in the robbery.

10   Q.   And you interviewed them?

11   A.   Falcón interviewed some of them.

12   Q.   What did you learn from the witnesses?

13   MR. ASHFORD: Objection. Ms. Foster is moving into hearsay.

14   THE COURT: Overruled.

15   MS. FOSTER: Do you need the question read back?

16   A.   No. I took descriptions of the suspect from three witnesses,
17   including Anthony Alteri, the owner of the restaurant, and two patrons.
18   One was Lew Levine; the other was Johnny Omar. Their descriptions of
19   the perpetrator were pretty similar—older guy; Caucasian, balding,
20   6–foot, 180 pounds, facial hair.

21   Q.   Did they tell you anything else about the suspect?

22   A.   Oh, yes. He carried a gym bag and told them to put all of their
23   belongings in the bag.

24   Q.   Did you and Detective Falcón compare notes at any point; I mean
25   did the victims he interviewed give a similar description?

26   MR. ASHFORD: Objection. This calls for obvious hearsay.

27   THE COURT: Ms. Foster, is the Detective going to testify?

28   MS. FOSTER: Yes.

29   THE COURT: I am going to allow the testimony. If there is a problem
30   afterwards, I will ignore the evidence.

31   MS. FOSTER: Thank you, Your Honor. Detective, so you compared
32   notes with Detective Falcón?

33   A.   Yes. The four folks he talked to all came up with a similar
34   description.

35   Q.   At that point, what did you do?

36   A.   I was pretty sure I knew who the perpetrator was based on the
37   description. I busted the defendant here before, for robbery, always the
38   same kind of MO.

39   Q.   But what did you do after you took the statements?

40   A.   I called back to the stationhouse and asked the duty sergeant to
41   organize a photo array and to include the defendant's photograph.

42   Q.   Did you keep that photo array?

A. I did.

Q. Before I ask you to show it to the court, did you direct the duty sergeant how to select the pictures in the photo array?

A. I told him to pick out older white guys, skinny, with facial hair. I told him to match the defendant as closely as possible.

MS. FOSTER: Your Honor, Mr. Ashford has already been provided with a copy of the photographs. I don't think that he objects to their introduction into evidence.

MR. ASHFORD: No objection, Your Honor. Of course, that does not mean that I agree that the array was a fair one.

THE COURT: Of course, that is understood.

MS. FOSTER: Detective, what happened next?

A: One of the patrol officers went back to the station to pick up the photo array.

Q. And once you had the photo array, what did you do?

A. I showed it to Alteri, Levine and Omar. Falcón and I agreed that the other people could leave and that we would get hold of them if we needed them.

Q. Did they identify the defendant?

A. Without difficulty, they sure did.

Q. Did you admonish, I mean warn the witnesses about any risks at this point?

MR. ASHFORD: Objection. The question is so broad; I am not sure what it means.

THE COURT: Well, I am pretty sure that the Detective knows. Over-ruled.

A. Sure. We tell witnesses the importance of getting the right person. We have no interest in arresting innocent people. So we tell people not to fake or force an ID. Like here, some of the folks just couldn't do it.

Q. Based on the statements that Misters Alteri, Levine and Omar made, what happened next?

A. I went home and went to bed.

Q. Nothing else that night?

A. I asked Detective Falcón if he would get a warrant to arrest the defendant and told him that I would meet him in the morning so that we could pick up the defendant.

Q. Did you pick up the defendant the next day?

A. Actually, I did not.

Q. Oh. Nothing else for now, Your Honor.

CROSS EXAMINATION

MR. ASHFORD: Good morning, Detective.

A. Hi.

1   Q. When you conducted your interview of Alteri, Omar and Levine,
2 ... wait, let me back up a second. Do you remember the time when you
3 finished up on the evening of April 6?

4   A. Probably around 10:30 or 11:00.

5   Q. And the original 911 call came in at 9:00, correct?

6   A. Yes.

7   Q. And you did not respond to the 911 call, did you, not right away?

8   A. That's right.

9   Q. So you were at the restaurant for maybe an hour or an hour and
10 a half at the longest, if my calculations are correct, isn't that correct?

11   A. I guess so; you did the calculations.

12   Q. They are not too difficult, Detective. If you got there at 9:30 and
13 went home around 10:30, that is one hour.

14   A. Yeah.

15   Q. So when you conducted the interview of the witnesses, they were
16 all in same room, weren't they?

17   A. The Three Pigs is a pretty big restaurant.

18   Q. But when you were interviewing, say, Alteri, where were Omar
19 and Levine, in hearing distance, weren't they? Or were you interviewing
20 them all together at one time?

21   A. At first, all of them were together when I got there. But I asked
22 each of them to move away so that I could interview them privately.

23   Q. So when one of them told you what the perpetrator looked like,
24 the other witnesses could not hear what was being said, is that your tes-
25 timony?

26   A. That is my testimony.

27   Q. Would you be surprised if the witnesses contradicted you?

28   A. Yes.

29   Q. You said that once you heard the description of the perpetrator,
30 you were pretty sure right away that it was the defendant because the
31 MO was unusual and similar to the defendant's MO, correct?

32   A. Yes.

33   Q. What is unusual about having victims put valuables in a gym
34 bag? Robbers must carry their loot in something, right?

35   A. Sure. But in my experience, gym bags are not the normal bag of
36 choice.

37   Q. Are Louis Vuitton handbags?

38   MS. FOSTER: Objection. Mr. Ashford is being argumentative.

39   THE COURT: Sustained. Mr. Ashford, you can make your point with-
40 out sarcasm, can't you?

41   MR. ASHFORD: I am sorry.

1   Q. Detective, based on your training and experience, what kind of
2 bags are typically used in robberies, ones where the perpetrator is taking
3 bulky property from a large number of victims?

4   A. All sorts of bags, shopping bags are common.

5   Q. Detective, I am not too familiar with Tres Porcellini. Would you
6 describe the décor?

7   A. It is an Italian place; it has about ten tables. It has a bar along
8 the western side of the restaurant.

9   Q. Is it well lighted?

10   A. I guess so.

11   Q. Well, wait. I saw an ad for the restaurant that said, come to Tres
12 Porcellini for intimate dining.

13   MS. FOSTER: Objection. I am not sure if Mr. Ashford is testifying,
14 but what foundation is there for his question?

15   THE COURT: Overruled. Detective, let me shorten the process here.
16 Are you familiar with the restaurant and how it advertises itself?

17   A. I am.

18   THE COURT: Have you ever eaten there?

19   A. Yes.

20   THE COURT: I think that Mr. Ashford is trying to get at the lighting
21 conditions in the restaurant. Do you have knowledge, personal knowl-
22 edge, of that?

23   A. A little.

24   THE COURT: Mr. Ashford, I am getting in your way. I was trying to
25 shorten the process, but you can get back to your cross examination.

26   MR. ASHFORD: You were very helpful, Your Honor. Detective, so
27 isn't the restaurant not well lit? Isn't it dimly lit so that couples can
28 engage in intimate dining?

29   A. I guess so.

30   Q. You didn't ask the witnesses how long the perpetrator was in the
31 restaurant, did you?

32   A. I did.

33   Q. What was their answer?

34   A. Five to ten minutes, something like that.

35   THE COURT: Mr. Ashford, I hate to interrupt. It is getting time for
36 a break. Are you almost done?

37   MR. ASHFORD: I am done. Oh, wait. One more thing, if I may ask
38 the Detective another question?

39   THE COURT: Okay. You have five more minutes and then we will
40 take a break.

41   Q. Detective, one thing seems odd. Usually robbers try to disguise
42 themselves, don't they?

1   A. Yes.

2   Q. Didn't the perpetrator try to disguise himself?

3   A. I don't know.

4   MR. ASHFORD: Nothing further.

5   (Court recessed)

6   THE COURT: Thank you, Mr. Ashford and Ms. Foster. I had to deal
7 with another matter. I think that you were both done with the Detective,
8 am I correct?

9   MS. FOSTER: Yes.

10   MR. ASHFORD: Yes.

11   THE COURT: Call your next witness, Ms. Foster.

12   MS. FOSTER: The People call Detective Martin Falcón.

13   Detective Martin Falcón was called as a witness, being duly sworn,
14 was examined and testified as follows:

15   DIRECT EXAMINATION

16   MS. FOSTER: Detective, would you please state your name for the
17 court and spell your name for the court reporter?

18   A. Martin Falcón. F–A–L–C–O–N.

19   Q. You currently serve as a detective with the McGeorge City Police
20 Department, is that correct?

21   A. Yes.

22   Q. How long have you held that position?

23   A. For three years.

24   Q. And how long have you been with the McGeorge City Police
25 Department?

26   A. I was hired in YR–8.

27   Q. Let me take you back to April 6, YR–01. Were you assigned to
28 investigate a report of an armed robbery at the Osteria Tres Porcellini?

29   A. I was, along with Detective Sergio.

30   Q. Do you remember what time you got to the scene of the robbery?

31   A. It was around 9:30 P.M.

32   Q. What did you do once you were there?

33   A. I followed Detective Sergio's instructions. He wanted to interview
34 the three witnesses who seemed to have had the best view of the defen-
35 dant. I took four victims upstairs to the business office and had three of
36 them wait outside while I interviewed each one.

37   Q. What information did the victims provide you?

38   A. Two of them did not get much of a view of the defendant. They
39 were frightened and tried not to look at him when he demanded their
40 valuables, and his face was partially obscured.

41   Q. But two of the victims did get a good view, didn't they?

1   A. Generally, they did.

2   Q. What did they tell you?

3   A. They both described a tall Caucasian, maybe 6', 6'3", 160–190
4   pounds.

5   Q. Anything else?

6   A. Not that I remember.

7   Q. Do you remember how long you were at the restaurant?

8   A. Well, about an hour. Sergio was done pretty quickly and called
9   up to me when he was done. He said that he knew who the perp was.

10   THE COURT: Detective, is there a reason why you stopped speaking?

11   A. I saw the defense attorney over there about to jump up. I didn't
12   want to keep talking if he was going to object.

13   THE COURT: Oh. Mr. Ashford, you were not going to make a hear-
14   say objection, were you?

15   MR. ASHFORD: No, Your Honor. I am waiting with baited breath to
16   hear the Detective's testimony.

17   THE COURT: Ms. Foster, back to your witness.

18   MS. FOSTER: Okay, so Detective Sergio indicated that he knew who
19   the perpetrator was and what happened then?

20   A. He called downtown for a photo array.

21   Q. And after it arrived, what happened?

22   A. I did, well, let me back up. Sergio told the other victims that they
23   could go home.

24   Q. Why was that?

25   A. They did not get a great look at the guy.

26   Q. Okay. But their description of the suspect was consistent with
27   the defendant's appearance, isn't that the case?

28   A. Definitely.

29   Q. Now, what did you do next in connection with this case?

30   A. After the owner and the two other victims identified our guy,
31   Sergio asked me to get an arrest warrant the next morning. He had too
32   much overtime already and needed some sleep.

33   Q. Did you get the warrant the next day?

34   A. I did.

35   Q. And after you secured the warrant, what did you do?

36   A. I knew where the defendant hung out, and I waited to spot him
37   on the street. I arrested him when I saw him.

38   Q. What did you do then?

39   A. I took him back to the restaurant. It's just in the same neighbor-
40   hood.

41   Q. What happened at the restaurant?

1   A.   I called ahead and asked if the owner was there yet. And he was.
2   So I spoke to him and told him that I had someone for him to look at.

3   Q.   And?

4   A.   When I got to the restaurant, Mr. Alteri was already outside,
5   waiting for me.

6   Q.   Did he identify the defendant?

7   A.   He did. He came right over to the car and without hesitation, he
8   said, that is him.

9   MS. FOSTER: Nothing further right now, Your Honor.

10   CROSS EXAMINATION

11   MR. ASHFORD: Detective, I want to go back to something you said a
12   few moments ago. You said that the four people whom you were inter-
13   viewing did not get a good view of the perpetrator, isn't that correct?

14   A.   That is correct.

15   Q.   And you interviewed each one separately, didn't you?

16   A.   Yes, I did. That is standard practice at the department.

17   Q.   That is to avoid one witness influencing another, isn't it?

18   A.   Yes, sir.

19   Q.   Oh, and you said something about the perpetrator's face, you
20   said that it was partially obscured, didn't you?

21   A.   I did.

22   Q.   Would you explain what you meant, it sounded like the perpetra-
23   tor had on a disguise of some kind? That was what you meant, wasn't it?

24   A.   One of the victims said that the defendant had a kerchief on his
25   face but that it fell off during the robbery.

26   Q.   Thank you, Detective. I think that I have just one or two more
27   questions for you. It sounds like you were really careful to follow depart-
28   mental procedure when you interviewed each witness separately. Do you
29   know if Detective Sergio followed the same procedure when he inter-
30   viewed the three witnesses downstairs in the restaurant?

31   A.   I have no idea, but I assume that he would follow protocol.

32   Q.   Oh? He was downstairs in the restaurant, wasn't he?

33   A.   Yes.

34   Q.   And from what I can tell and have seen going there a few times,
35   it is a small restaurant, maybe ten tables?

36   A.   I guess so.

37   Q.   So when he was interviewing the three witnesses who seem
38   ready to identify the defendant, they must have been within hearing dis-
39   tance of one another?

40   MS. FOSTER: Objection. The question calls for sheer speculation.
41   There are no facts in evidence that allow such a line of questions.

1   THE COURT: Mr. Ashford, I see where you are going, but I have to
2   sustain the objection.

3   MR. ASHFORD: Maybe I can clarify the matter. Okay, Detective, so
4   to the best of your knowledge, where were the three witnesses who stayed
5   downstairs, where were they when you went upstairs?

6   A.   They were at the bar.

7   Q.   They must have been upset, so maybe they were having a drink?

8   A.   The owner was there and he offered everybody a glass of Grappa
9   to help settle their nerves.

10   Q.   And again, to the best of your ability and within your personal
11   knowledge, where were the witnesses when you came back downstairs?

12   A.   They, well, Alteri and Levine were at the bar. Omar was talking
13   to Sergio.

14   Q.   I appreciate your candor, Detective. So one more question. You
15   follow protocol, as you indicated. But why didn't you follow protocol when
16   you did a one-on-one show up of the suspect when you brought the defen-
17   dant to the restaurant on morning of April 7?

18   A.   I don't understand your question. Our protocol says we take a
19   suspect back to the scene in a timely fashion to be sure that we have the
20   right perpetrator and to make sure that the victim or witness's memory
21   is still fresh.

22   Q.   What about when it is a day later and you already have an arrest
23   warrant?

24   MS. FOSTER: Objection. Even if a protocol exists, that is irrelevant
25   to the constitutional challenge that Mr. Ashford has raised.

26   THE COURT: Sustained. Mr. Ashford, I thought for sure you said
27   that you were done?

28   MR. ASHFORD: A few more questions, Your Honor.

29   THE COURT: Of course, go ahead.

30   MR. ASHFORD: Detective, you said that you called the restaurant
31   and told Alteri that you were bringing someone by for him to identify,
32   didn't you?

33   A.   Something like that.

34   Q.   Surely, if you recognize how suggestive your statement was, don't
35   you?

36   MS. FOSTER: Objection. The question is argumentative, it is hostile,
37   and it calls for speculation about a legal issue that is the question for the
38   Court to decide.

39   THE COURT: Sustained.

40   MR. ASHFORD: Nothing further, Your Honor.

41   THE COURT: Ms. Foster, do you need any redirect?

42   MS. FOSTER: I am done for now. I don't have additional witnesses at
43   this time either.

1   THE COURT: Mr. Ashford and Ms. Foster, is the photo array here? I
2 assume that you both want me to look at the photo array in deciding this
3 case?

4   MR. ASHFORD: I am sorry, Your Honor. I did not make a formal
5 motion to introduce the photo array. I will do so now.

6   THE COURT: Ms. Foster, I assume that you have no objection?

7   MS. FOSTER: Of course not.

8   THE COURT: Mr. Ashford, do you have anything else at this time?

9   MR. ASHFORD: Well, Your Honor, I wonder if Ms. Foster would
10 stipulate to Mr. Kirby's height and weight? That is part of the arrest
11 report that is a matter of public record.

12   MS. FOSTER: Stipulate, Your Honor.

13   MR. ASHFORD: Thank you, Ms. Foster. May the record reflect that
14 Mr. Kirby is 5′ 9″ in height, and he weighs 151 pounds?

15   THE COURT: Yes. Anything else, counsel?

16   MS. FOSTER: No, Your Honor.

17   MR. ASHFORD: I do want to raise one more concern. On this record,
18 I think that the photo array was unduly suggestive; the police made no
19 effort to get the defendant counsel, the one-on-one procedure was com-
20 pletely unnecessary and entirely suggestive. If you accept any of these
21 arguments, I would like to show that the eyewitnesses' trial testimony
22 should be excluded as well as their out-of-court identification.

23   THE COURT: We are going to adjourn. I will have my ruling after
24 lunch. If I find for Mr. Ashford, Ms. Foster, are you ready to proceed on
25 the other issues raised by Mr. Ashford?

26   MS. FOSTER: Yes, Your Honor.

VI. PEOPLE v. KIRBY: EYEWITNESS TESTIMONY AT TRIAL AND EXPERT TESTIMONY

For the next assignment, assume that Judge Bricker has found for the Defendant and suppressed all of the evidence with regard to the photo array and one-on-one show-up where Anthony Alteri identified the Defendant. This exercise shows you how, even if an out-of-court identification is improper, a witness may still be able to make an in-court identification.

Refer back to section II. *Overview of the Law.* In brief summary, the Court has held that the prosecution may use in-court identification evidence even if the trial court suppressed the out-of-court identification. In *Wade,* the Court held that the fruit-of-the-poisonous tree doctrine was applicable in such a case. In effect, if the trial court found that the in-court identification was not the product of the earlier procedure, the witness could identify the defendant in court.

Further, as you saw earlier, in his motion, Mr. Ashford asked for a pre-trial ruling on whether he would be allowed to call an expert who would testify about the risks inherent in eyewitness identification. If the case goes to trial, that issue becomes important. State courts have divided on the use of experts at trial to explain the risks inherent in eyewitness identifications. Courts are aware of the real risks of misidentification. Thus, despite the erosion of some of the constitutional protections that *Wade* and *Gilbert* seemed to promise, some courts have developed non-constitutional protections for criminal defendants.

This simulation is designed to allow your professor to assign you the role of prosecution or defense counsel. The simulation includes two related legal questions: first, given that the court found the out-of-court identifications inadmissible, may the prosecution introduce the witnesses' in-court identification? The Teacher's Manual includes role summaries for witnesses who will testify at the hearing. If your professor uses this simulation, he or she will give the role summaries to students to serve as the witnesses and assign students to serve as counsel.

The second part of the simulation involves the admissibility of expert testimony on the risks inherent in eyewitness identification. Courts have divided on the question. The question is a legal one. The Teacher's Manual includes a discussion of the case law and some cases and articles dealing with the topic. Depending on your professor's preference, you may be assigned to submit a memorandum of points and authorities on one side of the issue. Alternatively, you may be assigned to give an oral argument on the question.

†